SURVIVAL AND SOCIOLOGY

SURVIVAL AND SOCIOLOGY

Vindicating the Human Subject

Kurt H. Wolff

Transaction Publishers
New Brunswick (U.S.A.) and London (U.K.)

Copyright © 1991 by Transaction Publishers,
New Brunswick, New Jersey 08903

Library of Congress Catalog Number: 90-10802
ISBN: 0-88738-357-2
Printed in the United States of America

Library of Congress Cataloging-in-Publication Data

Wolff, Kurt H., 1912–
    Survival and sociology: vindicating the human subject/Kurt H. Wolff.
        p.   cm.
    ISBN 0-88738-357-2
    1. Sociology.   I. Title.
HM51.W62   1990
301—dc20   90-10802
                                                                CIP

0

Dedicated
to
Those This Book Speaks To

Contents

Preface

The fundamental question about sociology today that this book tries to confront is the same question that is to be asked about whatever activity you may be engaged in or contemplate: How can I, to the best of my conscience and consciousness, pursue this activity in the face of the unprecedented situation of humanity? Unprecedented, because for the first time in its history, humanity has at its disposal the knowledge to obliterate itself, all life, and its planet along with it. Must not everybody spend his or her life trying to prevent this, to preserve life? How does my activity, sociology, contribute to preserving life, rather than allowing its imperilment to continue? In fact, considering the relatively weak response to our many insanities—such as stockpiling arms, proliferating nuclear weapons and waste, causing ecological problems, increasing or ignoring the hardly graspable differences between rich and poor within and among societies—it sometimes seems that there is not only the feasibility of our suicide but its attraction, a longing for the end of it all.

For sociologists, the rational answer to the question of how to justify engaging in sociology appears obvious: we must engage in what sociology has always been best at, critically analyzing our society and on the basis of this analysis proposing alternatives. For the fundamental difference between sociologies past and present seems only to be that today's relevant society is not that of a given sociologist but the whole earth, the "global village."

I myself cannot accept this answer as a principle to act on. This answer takes it for granted that it is the rational answer: its understanding of rationality or reasonableness is traditional. But this rationality or reasonableness belongs to the same tradition that has at least not prevented us from sliding into our unprecedented crisis.

Here enter surrender. Surrender (in this context) is the maximally bearable *suspension of tradition*, for encountering one's problem or object or situation or partner or self in surrender is as unmediated an encounter as one can stand. The argument for surrender is based on the fact that the sum total of our traditions cannot be affirmed (or rejected), for not even their inspiring components have been strong enough to lead us elsewhere than where we are. In suspending tradition, surrrender tests it—tests it with the greatest rigor that a human being can muster, thus finding out what, at its most honest, he or she can truly believe. This outcome of surrender is its *catch*. Depending on what or whom I surrender to, the catch may be many things other than a truth that can be stated as a proposition—for instance, a change in personality, a decision, a product; but whatever the catch is, as a result of surrender it always is closer to the essence of what or whom I have surrendered to than is possible to attain in any other way. For this reason—this maximally attainable understanding—the human being today is at its *most rational* in surrender, that is, substantively rational (rather than functionally rational).

The components of this book are "catches" of surrenders to their various topics—to the very question of the justifiability of sociology today ("Sociology?")—and, to make this question and my answer to it more plausible, to that of the justifiability of another dimension of life, art ("Art Now?"); to the history of sociology ("A Sociological Approach to the History of Sociology"); to (aspects of) particular sociologists ("Scheler's Shadow on Us," "Into Alfred Schutz's World," "Karl Mannheim," "Anomie and the Sociology of Knowledge, in Durkheim and Today"); and, finally, to where I find myself as of the time of this writing on my initial question ("From Nothing to Sociology").

I call the components of this book *entries* rather than chapters (or sections or parts), for terms like these suggest a unilinearity that would misrepresent this text. Instead they represent aspects of a single concern—with sociology now. They are entries, widening and deepening into a conception and, simultaneously, practice of a sociology envisaged. Hence the term entry seems best to designate each of them, and in a second sense, too: as an entry into the log that charts the development of this sociology.

Instead of "entries," I could also have said "approaches," namely, to the fundamental question of the book, the last piece of which would then be entitled "preliminary arrival"—the point at which I have arrived as of this time. But I prefer the double meaning of "entry."

The thrust of this book is affirmative—although it does not necessarily affirm what a given reader, sociologist or nonsociologist, may expect. Instead, it is affirmative in a radical sense of "Die and become" (Goethe),

"Except a corn of wheat . . . die, it bringeth forth much fruit" (John 12: 24), "From nothing to sociology" (as the last entry, "A Transformation of the Entries," has it), because "The wind bloweth where it listeth" (John 3: 8), and can inspire or blow over (which is the same thing) a sociologist, too.

FIRST ENTRY
SOCIOLOGY?

FIRST ENTRY

Sociology?

I. Sociology and Its Time

Is there a place, a role, a function, indeed, is there any justification for sociology? If so, for what kind of sociology? The reason for asking this question may need to be spelled out, although actually it is as clear as anything that stares us in the face. The reason is simply this present human condition: for the first time in history there exists the possibility of the man-made end of all men, women, and children, of all life, of the entire planet itself.

For a few decades now, roughly a third as long as the word "sociology" is old, it has widely been unfashionable to practice sociology in reference to its time. We all know, however, that sociology so began and that for roughly its first hundred years it continued to be informed, inspired, bothered by the time in which it existed. Comte, who coined the word (to his honor, he apologized for its Latin-Greek misalliance), saw sociology as his messianic mission to bring his time to its proper self-consciousness, to the consciousness of having to be scientific. Marx, unlike Comte, did not look to history: he looked to its agents, into whom in a ferocious fight of and for secularization he transformed the stages of Hegel's Reason—the two classes that Marx perceived to be in definitive, if not eschatological, conflict, which must precede their suspension in freedom unknown, and unknowable prior to its advent. Spencer, comically at a distance from Marx and vying with Comte for originality, like Comte marshalled his interpretation of science—to celebrate his time, the time of the victory of Victoria, which promised forever bigger and better. Durkheim, instead, looked at his France and justified sociology by exploring the puzzling rates of suicide, which led him to discover anomie. Simmel discovered something similar, which

3

he called the conflict and the tragedy of culture, and in the face of which he left sociology for an ontological philosophy of life, or more precisely, a *lebensphilosophische* ontology.

The shift away from the practice of a sociology that had such relations to its time, or rather the banishment of such relations from the theory of sociology, but its perseverance in the practice itself, exacerbated a conflict between theory and practice until it came to a head most patently and frighteningly in Max Weber, who was quite conscious of it. The *locus classicus* of this conflict and Weber's consciousness of it is the famous passage at the end of *The Protestant Ethic*:

> No one knows who will live in this cage [which had become of the Puritan's 'light cloak'] in the future, or whether at the end of this tremendous development entirely new prophets will arise, or there will be a great rebirth of old ideas and ideals, or, if neither, mechanized petrification, embellished with a sort of convulsive self-importance. For of the last stage of this cultural development, it might well be truly said: "Specialists without spirit, sensualists without heart; this nullity imagines that it has attained a level of civilization never before achieved,"[1]

> But [Weber at once checks himself] this brings us to the world of judgments of value and of faith, with which this purely historical discussion need not be burdened. [This remarkable translation, incidentally, is by Talcott Parsons.]

Since this tortuous conflict broke out in Max Weber and was suppressed by him, it has once more largely been ignored, and what may be called Max Weber's official side has been invoked and put into practice by official sociology, at least in the United States. But there has been another kind of sociology, an opposition party, that goes back, more or less directly and faithfully, to Marx and is at any rate true to the early history of sociology, concerned with a diagnosis of its time. Among the most obvious representatives of this sociology of the minority are Karl Mannheim in Germany and England and C. Wright Mills in the United States.

II. "What Poetry after Auschwitz?"

The question raised about sociology applies, of course, to *all* human activities, for if we disappear, nothing that anyone does makes sense. But to give up sociology or anything else which at least is not destructive is a counsel of despair, a confirmation and acceptance of the situation as hopeless. As far as sociology is concerned, the more hopeful position is to ask what *kind* of sociology might contribute to averting the end, for the end is not foredoomed.

Thus formulated, the question suggests its answer: the kind of sociology that might contribute to averting our end analyzes circumstances that have led to our crisis and helps overcome it, in other words, a historically pragmatic sociology, in the most obvious sense of "pragmatic." But if our question, Is there a place, a role, a function, is there any justification for sociology? reminds us of the question, What poetry after Auschwitz? then there also emerges a big difference between the two.

Those who ask, What poetry after Auschwitz? have never been in Auschwitz or are among the few who have survived it, and the answer seems clear: we are morally, even ontologically, enjoined to write poetry after Auschwitz, if we would not only come to terms with our inexperience or our survival, but prove worthy of either our inexperience or our survival of Auschwitz. And indeed, everybody now writes, or can write, poems—*but as if there had been no Auschwitz!* By contrast, we cannot count on there being any survivor or anyone who has no experience of the bomb once the bomb goes off. And what is more, Auschwitz has occurred, but the last bomb, unlike the horror over Hiroshima and Nagasaki (dropped by order of a good democrat from Missouri) has not gone off yet.

III. World-Opening and Critical Sociology

Many people, including sociologists, probably do not think about the present state of the human condition in the terms here presented. A different way of thinking is implied if the question "Sociology?" does not come up at all, because it is taken for granted that sociology should continue at its most relevant, namely, uncovering the causes of misery and the ways of weakening or eliminating them. Today, more specifically, sociology should uncover those features of society that breed the dangers of our suicide and those other elements and measures that weaken or eliminate these features. I honor such a view and rejoice in its being held and acted upon; it surely sounds reasonable and rational and indeed is what I earlier described as a "historically pragmatic" view. But I will explain why I myself cannot act on it. It is that the unprecedentedness of our crisis makes me distrust such a received, such a "precedented" conception of reasonableness and rationality, in the same way as it makes me distrust our traditions, which, after all, have brought us to where we are.

How, then, must I answer my question in such a situation? It took me some time before I made a connection between my search and the fact that some sociology I was reading did not make me feel indifferent or bored, but excited me, made me feel it was important, so that the question, "Sociology?" disappeared. Then I proceeded by induction.

The first two pieces I read were quite dissimilar. One was a dissertation that consisted largely of transcripts of interviews with—by a strange coincidence!—survivors of the Holocaust.[2] I could not, and cannot, understand how these individuals survived, even how their interviewer managed to survive their stories. I felt the writing was a necessary record, or an absolute record (like *Let Us Now Praise Famous Men*)[3] in the face of which history and its questions vanished. The other very different piece of writing was a description of what it is like to be a machinist;[4] it struck me as being in the best tradition of the Chicago School, and the Chicago School has impressed me ever since I first became acquainted with it as an excellent kind of sociology. I asked myself what these two works had in common that I found so gripping, and realized that both of them introduced readers into worlds they had not known before.

But *all* readers? Fellow survivors and machinists, too? For them, I suppose, it is not so much an introduction to a world they do not know as a having made clear and distinct to them what they in some way do know, being told the truth about it: a shock of recognition. To be able to have such an effect indicates, I should think, the artistic component of a sociology that is viable and lasting, something to which Robert Redfield alerted readers many years ago in a paper with a somewhat provocative title, "The Art of Social Science,"[5] in which he presents as examples de Tocqueville's *Democracy in America*, Veblen's *Theory of the Leisure Class*, and Sumners *Folkways*.

But if what these two studies, of Holocaust survivors and a machinist's life, share is the opening up of a world, new to their readers or recognized by them with a shock, there was, and is, another kind of sociology that makes me forget the question of its justification: the sociology that is critical of its society, including some of the writings of the Frankfurt School, of Mannheim and Mills, or of Gouldner, and many others. And here I want to mention another dissertation I have read recently on the war in Vietnam (since published).[6] This has convinced me that the fundamental assumption underlying American strategy was that of Vietnamese technological backwardness, an assumption that made it unthinkable, beyond the horizon of imagination, that the Vietnamese could possibly win. I consider this study an example of critical sociology, and exasperating in its sober, detailed description.

But now, I asked myself, what is it that makes these two kinds of sociology—let me call them world-opening and critical—so worthwhile and so convincing? What is it that they have in common?

IV. Vindicating the Human Subject

I think what both kinds of sociology have in common is the insistence on the *subject*,[7] the recall, the vindication, the celebration of the subject at a time when the subject has been made into a thing by bureaucracy, snuffed out by totalitarianism, and when it will be destroyed physically if the threat from which this book issues becomes fact—the last fact. This is the reason why this threat, why history itself vanishes for me in the reading of these sociological writings: it is an encounter with fellow human beings, an overwhelming presence, a present that no longer is different from past and future, but annuls temporal distinctions: it is "out of time," out of this world, thus accessible to all times.

But what is the connection between such atemporality or ahistoricity and the relation to its time which I claimed gave rise to sociology and inspired it during its first century? However different from each other, the three examples I have given—the study of survivors, of a machinist, of the war in Vietnam—make *present*, make us confront, aspects of our time, worlds that figure in our time which we did not know or recognize in their very nature or essence. To use a phenomenological term, their *eidos* on reading about them overwhelms us, whatever our other feelings, and our other feelings are surely quite different in the three cases. What we are faced with are historical realities, thrown up by history. In comparison to *this* relation to our time—for it *is* a relation to our time— that of classical sociology appears simple, naive, and innocent, and it was: there is our time, there are features of it that are bad or evil or threatening or wrong, and here is my effort to explain and change them. Today, it seems, we need to transcend the world of history, of everyday, if we would have any chance to recognize it.

To the extent that this is so, sociology, once again, shows a feature it shares with art. But art is only the best-known occasion for being fully absorbed by an encounter; and to be fully absorbed does away with the temporal dimension, indeed with all orientation that we need and use to get on in the everyday world. "Out of this world" means out of the world of everyday life, but into that world that absorbs us.

But there is a difference between sociology and art, as well as many other occasions of absorption. This difference characterizes not so much the absorption itself as the reemergence from it into the world of everyday life, into the *Lebenswelt*, into what Alfred Schutz called "the world of paramount reality."[8] Traditionally, sociology has explored this world, for, unlike philosophy or art, it is born in it, and the everyday world is its home. It has sought to understand how society ticks, but can this still be its aim today, when we do not know whether the ticking is perhaps a countdown? Even for people who are not sociologists, what attitude toward the paramount reality is called for today? Today, when everybody willy-nilly contributes to that chimera of a national security, when everybody is employed as a patriot,[9] when we take it for granted that the news of famine is interrupted by a commercial break, followed by another "human interest" story, and when so-called elected representatives fall for science-fiction weapons and approve plans to divert revenue previously allocated for school luncheons and other nourishment? If we (whether we are sociologists or not, but especially if we are sociologists) trust our senses rather than the received notions that blind them, and thus us, to reality, the only way we can come to terms with our "paramount reality" is to say "No" to it, as Herbert Marcuse put it, for "'The whole is the truth,' and the whole is false."[10]

Thus, after having been absorbed by sociology, rather than by art or another occasion, we reemerge into the everyday world wanting to do something in this world that contributes to averting our end, to increasing the chance of the human condition to survive its fatal danger, and to emancipate itself from it and from the flaws of its antecedents.

Notes

1. Among (inconclusive) inquiries into the origin of this quotation within the quotation, see among others Stephen A. Kent, "Weber, Goethe, and the Nietzschean Allusion: Capturing the Source of the 'Iron Cage' Metaphor," *Sociological Analysis*, 44, 4 (1983): 297–319, esp. 301–2; see also Wolfgang Mommsen, "Max Weber's Political Sociology and His Philosophy of World History," in *Max Weber*, ed. Dennis Wrong (Englewood Cliffs: Prentice-Hall, 1970), pp. 183–94, esp. 186; and Alan Sica, "Reasonable Science, Unreasonable Life: The Happy Fictions of Marx, Weber, and Social Theory," in *A Weber-Marx Dialogue*, ed. by Robert J. Antonio and Ronald M. Glassman (Lawrence: University Press of Kansas, 1985), pp. 68–88, esp. 71–4, 85. (My thanks to Stephen Kalberg for alerting me to the latter two references.)
2. Henry Greenspan, "Who Can Retell? On the Recounting of Life History by Holocaust Survivors," (Ph.D. diss., Brandeis University, 1985).
3. James Agee and Walker Evans, *Let Us Now Praise Famous Men* (Boston: Houghton Mifflin, 1941).
4. Roger Tulin, *A Machinist's Semi-Automated Life* (San Pedro, CA: Singlejack Books, 1984).
5. Robert Redfield, "The Art of Social Science," *American Journal of Sociology* 54 (1948): 181–90.
6. James William Gibson, *The Perfect War: Technowar in Vietnam* (Boston, New York: Atlantic Monthly Press, 1986).
7. This became clear to me in a conversation with Robbie Pfeufer Kahn, to whom I am grateful.
8. Alfred Schutz, "On Multiple Realities" (1945), in *Collected Papers*, vol.

1, ed. and introd. Maurice Natanson (The Hague: Nijhoff, 1962), pp. 207–59.

9. For this formulation and for the contrast between ticking and countdown a few lines back, I am indebted to Jonathan B. Imber and thank him for permitting me their use.

10. Herbert Marcuse, "Preface: A Note on Dialectic" (1960), in *Reason and Revolution: Hegel and the Rise of Social Theory* (1941) (Boston: Beacon, 1960), p. xvi.

SECOND ENTRY
ART NOW?

Art Now?

I will now present a case paralleling that of and for sociology, the case of and for art. One reason is to make my claim that what applies to sociology also applies to any other activity more compelling. Another reason is my own commitment, not only to sociology (which originated in my student days, when Karl Mannheim introduced me to it), but also to art. This would be of no interest to readers and of no relevance to my present concern were it not that what thrust this book may have derives not only from its argument but also from its arguer: to submit to you "Art Now?" is another instance of the subject's relevance to discourse—of the vindication of the subject, which so pervades both the preface and "Sociology?"

I. Who Asks: "Art Now?"

The "now" in "art now?" refers, of course, to after Auschwitz and before that which has never in man's history been so uncertain. The question, art now? asks whether other activities that would more likely help avert a horrible future, even the end of it, and would instead contribute to bringing about a future that is better for man to survive in—whether such activities are more urgent than making art or enjoying art and thus whether they must have priority over art. If this is the question, then those activities, whatever they may be, and art compete for the little time we may have to shape a future. (How can you fiddle while Rome burns?)

Who asks this question? First, some types of persons—surely the vast majority—who do *not* ask it. There is the type (with many subtypes) who is not worried enough about the future for questions concerning it to interfere with his or her making or enjoying art. The second type is a person who is convinced that if art (making or enjoying it) were shortchanged, the future wouldn't be worth having anyway. Third is the individual whose concern with art is too slight to compete with the concern over the future. Finally, and perhaps most common, there is the type who doesn't care enough about either future or art for the question to come up. And there may be other types.

Who *is* exercised by the question? Obviously the type who is the opposite of the last: the individual who cannot let go of either concern, with either art or the future. If the two are about equal, such a person may divide the time and energy available equally between them. Such a person is very different from a second type to whom the question matters: the individual who is torn between the two, devotion to art and devotion to the future, and who does not know what to do. In the search for an answer such an individual has to become clearer about a number of things: What he or she means by art; what by the many problems, physical, political, economic, social, moral, that choke the future; what by priorities of concern. He or she wants to find out what to do for one of two reasons or both: because of the realization of having to do it, or because of wanting to do it, or, ideally, because of wanting to do what this individual realizes he or she *must* do. But more accurately, this human being cannot possibly do simply what he or she wants to do, because then there would be no question: he or she would act on his/her concern for the future (thus being the third type among those who do *not* ask the question) or would act on his/her concern with art (the second type).

The one now under discussion—the person who wants to find out what it is necessary to do because of the realization of having to do it— this type has only two wishes between whose fulfillment to choose: to justify what this person wants to do, concern himself with the future or with art; or to find out which of them must be followed even without his/her wanting to. Now this mere realization of what a person wants to do is eliminated as a reason for doing it: the *wanting to* can figure only as a justified want, one that has its right in the face of the uncertainty of the future or the power of art.

II. Cyrano de Bergerac

But is this an accurate description?

I am now going to report on an experience in another world, out of another world, than the one in which we were just now.

For it happened. I was watching the news during the war in Vietnam, which showed the rich people of Phnom Penh sitting in sidewalk cafés and playing tennis while the others, which is almost all, were poor, shelled, rocketed, wounded, starved, or killed. Yet the rich were convincing the president of the United States of America to send a few hundred million dollars more to postpone the destruction of the city so they wouldn't have to escape to their rivieras for another few weeks (the disaster of U.S. foreign policy was to be perpetuated in the name of morality while ending the disaster was immoral). Only a few hours after this news show I was entirely absorbed in watching *Cyrano de Bergerac*, jubilating in the art of acting, marveling at unbelievable love. And then, not reflecting as I am about to now, I went to my room, seeking out and finding a long novel I had written in 1933, more than half a century ago, during the first summer after Hitler's conquest of Germany. It was the last thing I did before leaving what had been my country. I then lived in the world of art, lived art, just like Rostand and just like my absorption with him during the massacres in Cambodia and Vietnam, whose rich had their counterpart in Germany and still do everywhere. But I had not looked at what I had written in 1933 (with the same absorption with which I had sat watching *Cyrano* and returned to that writing after this experience)—I had not looked at it for many years, even decades. But after watching *Cyrano* on television I read a chapter, "Joachim [I had even forgotten his name!] makes a poem." I had remembered it as a crucial chapter, a rendering of my way of being, but I had forgotten all except that the most extraordinary if not extravagant circumstances signaled the emergence of the poem. I had forgotten that Joachim, serenely occupying a bench on a hilltop, was visited by a sphinx, which was both human and an automaton, that they engaged in a dialogue, but that at the same time she was teasing him with a basket full of fruit that she held in one of her hind paws and a decanter full of wine that she held in the other but in such a manner that his grabbing activated its withdrawal, and the faster he tried the more the mechanism was accelerated. I had also forgotten that Joachim was not alone but buoyed up, if not carried, by others, three young people (of my own age then, while Joachim was old, that is, in his prime—and he was modeled after an adored friend, a poet who has long since died [when he was not yet fifty]), two young men and a woman. All, of course, had fallen in love with him, though in different ways, on his unexpected visit (I didn't leaf through earlier pages to see whether the four had known each other before Joachim's visit to their "house in the meadow" or if they met there). The relationship among the three people was loose, and Joachim was a genius, so everything moved ahead except that he frightened them by putting on an act of madness, which made them go pale. That made him laugh at and with the children, who couldn't distinguish fake from real insanity. They now were embarrassed because they of course had considered themselves art experts, and yet had not seen that the madness, whether fake or real, was the labor preceding the birth of the poem—which occurred as much to Joachim's surprise as to theirs, as well as to my own, who of course wrote it.[1]

III. "Art Now?" Is Stacked in Favor of Art

What precedes *was* written in another world, out of another world than the world we began in, which was the world of everyday life. The question "art now?" arose in the world of everyday life where a person may ask whether he/she should be occupied with art or with the future: it is in this world that both figure (among many other things). In the world of art, which is the one we just visited, one of them, the future, does not exist: there is—typically speaking—no future, hence no question of any future, because the artist and the enjoyer of art are wholly absorbed by art (as similarly by other things in other worlds); so they look neither forward nor back nor indeed in any direction outside art. While watching *Cyrano de Bergerac* and looking for that novel and finding and reading it, I was aware of no impending disaster, no Cambodia or Washington, hence no attending problems.

I must discuss more accurately, more honestly, than I did in the beginning the types who ask about "art now," who ask whether in view, however dim, of the threatening future, activities other than art must come first (in case art is to come at all). For I now wonder whether I know anybody who represents one or the other of the two types I thought of: the one who cannot let go of either art or the future and will be occupied with both; the other who is torn between the two, and, in fact, instead of following either tries to find which of them to follow, what to do. To my surprise I must answer that I do not know people who represent either type. How, then, did I hit on them? It was, I realize, by schematically deriving them from the types I imagined do not raise the question: the ones who are not worried enough about the future; those who won't have a future without art; those not concerned with art; and those who can't help but create it or love it otherwise. Hence the types who do ask the question must be those who are concerned with both and can either find room for them or cannot let go of either and in their turmoil feel abandoned to the question, which is the question of what they must do.

What happened then when to relax after this exercise in establishing types I watched a play, was moved out of the world of everyday life, the mundane world, into that of art, and in introducing my report on this asked whether what I had said was so? Now I am returning to this question, and I come closer to recognizing how it is than when I started out.

The first step in this approximation, just taken, was to realize that I know nobody who represents either of the two types who I said ask the question (although, like everybody else, I am sure I know representatives of each of the four who do not ask it; most of them are of the first type, those who are not worried enough about the future to ask, and of the third type, those who don't ask the question because they are not concerned enough about art). I now take a second step by recognizing that the question art now? is stacked in favor of art. For its more honest and precise formulation is: am I allowed to occupy myself with art, or am I not because I must devote myself to the future? It is a variant of the question, what poetry after Auschwitz? To show how stacked it is, exchange the verbs (or the objects) and recognize that quite a different question results: am I allowed to occupy myself with the future, or am I not because I must devote myself to art? I cannot think of one asking *this* question unless it be two lovers during an art class or one who must finish writing a short story before going on the trip long waited for or any other case of enforced occupation with art that delays a preferred state or activity.

What do we learn from this consideration about art, the future, and their relation?

IV. Rockbottom

First, the question, in the way it is stacked, comes out of a tradition in which art is considered of the essence of man; making and enjoying art is part of the life that is worthy of man, if not indispensable to it. This eliminates enforced preoccupation with art (a non sequitur suggested by the last examples) from our consideration. Second, the future is the future of humanity, as was implied in the very first sentence of this examination, not the future of any individual, family, or group, no matter how large, not even a nation. This obviously cannot mean that it is mankind who asks the question here since only individuals can, and one of them is asking it here in the sense that is in the process of being articulated. Third, if these two matters are clear and simple, the next, the relation between art and future is not. It requires the clarification of the factors that affect the future of humanity. They fall into two broad classes, human and nonhuman. Of many of the former—technological, economic, social, political, moral—we have a depressing view in Robert L. Heilbroner's *An Inquiry into the Human Prospect*,[2] frighteningly updated in Jonathan Schell's *The Fate of the Earth*.[3] The nonhuman factors may be summed up under the term climatic and range from changes toward more frequent and more widespread drought, antici- pated perhaps by the southward drift of the Sahara or the irregularity of the monsoons, for instance, to another ice age, little or big, possibly within our or our children's lifetimes. Of course, the two classes of factors are related in so far as human beings can do something not only about themselves but also, and with perhaps even greater consequences, about nature, that is, about the nonhuman factors of the future, and have done so since their beginning. What to do about both classes of factors covers all the activities that compete with art for our concern.

But might art itself be one of them? Is it possible to argue that it must have priority by the very criterion of helping to "avert a horrible future, even the end of it," and "to contribute to bring about a future that is better for man to survive in?" If so, art must be made with this prob- lematic future in mind. There may well be individuals for whom the answer to the question "art now?" is the effort to create a work of art in such a perspective. They might do it in the form of a novel or painting or other art form "with a purpose"—what in Germany in the 1920s was called a *Tendenzroman* or a *Tendenzstück*, and so on, or a didactic piece, a *Lehrstück*. This art, of which Bertolt Brecht is the best-known and best representative, aimed at showing features of contemporary society, above all negative features, to alert and warn those who were blind to them. ("Socialist realism," too, of course, is *Tendenzkunst*, but not so much critical as celebratory.) In this art, the future was more implied than it was the explicit frame of reference, which was the pre- sent. Walter Benjamin, who admired Brecht, went so far as to argue that "the correct political tendency of a work includes its literary quality because it includes its literary tendency," which in turn depends on its literary technique.[4] This strikes me as plausible also for a work of art that is explicitly oriented toward the future—as long as we deal with the type of art that is quite consciously intended by its maker to do something about man's future. On the other hand, there is art that is not planned but that overcomes the artist, but since there is hardly anything to be done to bring it to life, it can be no more than a vague consolation. Of course, once it occurs or is recalled, like the poem I fancied occurred to Joachim, it has consequences as all events do. Thus, the memory of Joachim's poem has had consequences for my present enterprise.

But there is another aspect of the future: am I responsible for it? Did my ancestors worry about the present generation? Most of them in all likelihood did not, and those who did surely extended their concern, not to all of humanity, but only to the successors of their own group—their family, tribe, class, race. Yet even today, to ask "art now?" is to ask a question that is raised by only a few types of persons, as we saw, moreover by persons typically of a socioeconomic status with a culture that allows or prompts them to ask such a question. Nevertheless, the question concerns all of humanity—the part about the future directly, that about art more indirectly. And the situation of the audience who hears the question parallels that of the askers: typically its members are persons who resemble the askers socioeconomically and culturally; but again, those outside the audience, too, are involved, directly or indirectly.

The reason there is the question whether we are to be held responsible for our successors is that we have learned to think farther ahead than did, presumably, most members of most past generations, and hence this question is one of the items on our agenda, possibly for the first time in human history. Compared with the question what to do *now*, however, even though the answer to it affects those who come after us, that of our responsibility to them must be postponed. But is the best we can do for them not in any case the best we can do *now*? If so, all we have to know is what is best now. What must I do—including devoting myself to art or to the future? I am back where I started, asking the question art now?

And I have no answer—except a personal one. But having gone to so much trouble only to be brought to the beginning, I feel I have reached rockbottom, that is, as real a beginning as I can reach on this occasion. Another way of saying this is to hope, even trust, that my personal answer is not idiosyncratic but of interest also to others, that it is to some extent representative. My answer, my report is: I try my best answering the question about art now. I do what I've got to do, that is, I practice my habitual occupations, which includes intermittently asking myself about my occupations from various perspectives. But what about art? Whatever my occupation, art is a part of me. I feel undernourished without it, without after a time reading fiction, hearing music, looking at paintings. I then forget the problematic character of my occupations, the everyday world, because I am in the world of art. This may suggest art as therapy but it is no more therapy than love, wisdom, goodness, and justice are: of course, all of these and other things do good, increase health, help sanity, give support, and may heal, but therapy is not of their essence. It throws no light on them to say that they are therapeutic, unless one were to argue that the human condition is a sickness, but even then, art, love, wisdom, goodness, and justice are intrinsic to it, and to call them elements of the sickness of the human condition is no more than to make a noise at a far distance.

More people who have thought about art than not probably take it to be an intrinsic part of society, even though not all would agree on the reason for it, for instance, its concern "with the mystery of existence in the human and metaphysical sense." [5] There probably has never been a society and there certainly has never been any humanity in which there was no art, and it is on the assumption that in this respect the future will be like the past that it makes sense to discuss the nature, the functions, the consequences, the relations of art. I am talking from a point of view that does not make this assumption but questions it.

Art, like religion and some other presumably universal social institutions may indeed be universal, but this means in societies. My question, art now? is based on the uncertainty of there being any society in a relevant, near future. Instead of art, I thus could have asked the same question about those other institutions. If Rome burns, "to fiddle" refers to all activities except fire-fighting (and saving oneself, since suicide won't save Rome either).

There is a deeper reason for raising the question with regard to art than in regard to religion or philosophy, for instance. For the fundamental question, as we found out before, is: What must I do? It is an existential, moral, political question, not an artist's question. The deeper reason emerged when I reported on my sudden recollection, after watching *Cyrano de Bergerac*, of a novel I had written many years earlier, on my relief and delight of a visit to the world of art. This made the problem worse since I had come out of that world again, while the question had remained. Yet, I felt strengthened; somehow, the question art now? had less urgency. I had been prepared to bear, even to affirm, my having only a personal answer to it. This affirmation came after I thought of our responsibility to our successors and asked whether the best we can do for them is the best we can do now, and I found myself back at the beginning question about art now, what to do now.

"But having gone to so much trouble," I felt, "only to be brought to the beginning, I feel I have reached rockbottom, that is, as real a beginning as I can reach on this occasion." I must not unduly suffer from the fact that I have not been able to say more on this occasion than I have, for the beginning I have made goes beyond itself, bearing on my life and your lives, whoever you are, unpredictably.

Notes

1. Wolff, "Joachim verfasst ein Gedicht," a chapter in the unpublished novel *Organda* (1933), has since been published in *Das Unumgängliche: Gedichte,*

Prosa, Theater, Essays ([Darmstadt:] Gesellschaft Hessischer Literatur-freunde, 1988), pp. 56–64.

2. Robert L. Heilbroner, *An Inquiry into the Human Prospect* (New York: Norton, 1974).

3. Jonathan Schell, *The Fate of the Earth* (New York: Knopf, 1982).

4. Walter Benjamin, "Der Autor als Produzent" (1934), in *Versuche über Brecht* (Frankfurt: Suhrkamp, 1966), pp. 96–7, 98.

5. Herbert Read, "Rational Society and Irrational Art," in *The Critical Spirit: Essays in Honor of Herbert Marcuse*, ed. by Kurt H. Wolff and Barrington Moore, with the assistance of Heinz Lubasz, Maurice R. Stein, and E. V. Walter (Boston: Beacon, 1967), p. 211.

THIRD ENTRY
A SOCIOLOGICAL APPROACH TO THE HISTORY OF SOCIOLOGY

A Sociological Approach to the History of Sociology

I. Surrender-and-Catch and Sociology

The "rockbottom" beginning I felt (and feel) I had reached, that is, the essay "Art Now?" itself, is the catch of my surrender to the question "art now?", fed by which further thinking could take off. But since I wrote this essay (already in the 1970s), I have instead thought further about surrender-and-catch and about sociology, and my thinking about the one is bound to have influenced my thinking about the other. You might find this even more obvious than it is to me. In this book, the influence of preoccupation with surrender-and-catch on sociology is far more pronounced than the influence of sociology on surrender-and-catch. As far as I can make out (at the present time), this preponderant influence shows itself as follows.

The individual's extreme, maximally bearable concentration which surrender is infuses the sociology here developing with the vindication of the subject, not only against the anti-human elements pervading (industrial and "postindustrial") society, but also for its own sake—the celebration of the subject, as the source of the future of humanity, if there is to be any human future. This sociology is inspired by those characteristics of the human being that are exclusively human: the human spirit and its manifestations, among them philosophy, poetry, art, religion, verbal language and other kinds of symbolism, and all the feelings associated with these. As to sociology, its studies focus on the relations between these and other exclusively human features and a feature or features of the society in which they are found. Societies or their features, like human beings, are mixed phenomena in the sense of having both exclusively human characteristics and characteristics they share with other animals, plants, even inorganic matter. For instance, differences in bodily strength are found among nonhuman animals and plants, but in man they are, except in situations where "man acts like a brute," expressed culturally. Yet having to work with nature—the biological organism, the earth and its atmosphere—culture itself is a mixed phenomenon. The sociology envisaged here is not in the service of social forces—such as power, even in its exclusively human forms, money and many kinds of technology—that are found among nonhuman animals too.

A second related feature of our emerging sociology is that it is a response to its historically unprecedented time, which it diagnoses as threatening humanity and its habitat and entrusts the individual with their survival and humanization; it trusts nothing but the individual if this survival and humanization are to be brought about. Surrender taught this sociology, so to speak, that the individual is at the same time, and inseparably, both most itself, that is, unique, and representative of humanity, or universal, *in surrender*—in a condition in which the maximum of relevant traditions or received notions that the individual can bear gets suspended.

II. Max Weber and His Society

Among the many implications of such a sociology is a revised conception of the history of sociology. What in this field (as well as in many others) is generally considered the best writing distinguishes itself by accuracy and reliability, by a loving devotion to detail; and such *Andacht zum Kleinen* is surely one of the glories of the *Geisteswissenschaften* (the Teutonic-sounding term, incidentally, coined by the German translator of John Stuart Mill's "moral sciences," the topic of Book V of *A System of Logic*). Indeed, it is probably still rare that a person does not respect or admire a scholar of the social sciences or the humanities who devotes the attention of a lifetime to ascertaining facts, no matter how trivial or even meaningless they might appear to one who does not know such passionate devotion, which, however, has the authority of a hallowed craft and is celebrated in Max Weber's famous and extraordinary lecture of 1918, *Science as a Vocation*—which has turned out to be so symptomatic and so prophetic.

According to Weber,

> whoever lacks the capacity to put on blinders, so to speak, and to come up
> to the idea that the fate of his soul depends upon whether or not he makes

the correct conjecture at this passage of this manuscript may as well stay away from science. He will never have what one may call the "personal experience" of science. Without this strange intoxication, ridiculed by every outsider; without this passion, this "thousands of years must pass before you enter into life and thousands more wait in silence"—according to whether or not you succeed in making this conjecture; without this, you have *no* calling for science and you should do something else.[1]

But Weber also says that science cannot tell us how we should live. What is symptomatic of his conception of science, including, of course, social science ("of course" rather for Weber and his innumerable followers), is that it reflects a significant trait of the society out of which Weber spoke, a society that included university students who were shocked by the defeat and misery of their country. This trait is the weakening of a generally internalized moral order. Weber said as much when he spoke of

> the need of some modern intellectuals to furnish their souls with, so to speak, guaranteed genuine antiques. In doing so, they happen to remember that religion has belonged among such antiques, and of all things religion is what they do not possess. By way of substitute, however, they play at decorating a sort of domestic chapel with small sacred images, from all over the world, or they produce surrogates through all sorts of psychic experiences to which they ascribe the dignity of mystic holiness, which they peddle in the book market. . . . This is plain humbug or self-deception.[2]

For in reality, only "the demon who holds the fibers of his very life"[3] can tell the individual how to live and what to do.

Weber, however, does not find it necessary to tell us more about this demon, nor does he instruct us on how to distinguish it from individual taste, preference, or whim. He must have taken it for granted that everybody grasped the distinction, just as he must have taken it for granted that everybody knew the difference between the ethic of ultimate ends (*Gesinnungsethik*) and fanaticism, and the difference between the ethic of responsibility (*Verantwortungsethik*) and opportunism; for, in his equally extraordinary *Politics as a Vocation* of the same year, Weber declared that "an ethic of ultimate ends is [not] identical with irresponsibility, . . . an ethic of responsibility is [not] identical with unprincipled opportunism. Naturally nobody says that."[4] And further:

> it is immensely moving when a *mature* man—no matter whether old or young in years—is aware of a responsibility for the consequences of his conduct and really feels such responsibility with heart and soul. He then acts by following an ethic of responsibility and somewhere he reaches a point where he says: "Here I stand; I can do no other." That is something genuinely

human and moving. And every one of us who is not spiritually dead must realize the possibility of finding himself at some time in that position. In so far as this is true, an ethic of ultimate ends and an ethic of responsibility are not absolute contrasts but rather supplements, which only in unison constitute a genuine man.[5]

Weber seems not to have suspected that many were *not* aware of the difference between demon and taste, the ethic of ultimate ends and fanaticism, and the ethic of responsibility and opportunism. He could not have predicted that a few years after his symptomatic and prophetic lectures there would arise so devastating a figure as Adolf Hitler, both a gigantic fanatic and a gigantic opportunist, who in his fanaticism and opportunism seduced and destroyed millions of people.

In not being conscious of the importance of explicating and driving home the differences between demon and taste and between the two ethics, Weber bore witness to the degree to which in his society these differences had lost their cognitive and normative hold, the degree to which there was an increasing tendency to idolize science, that is, to attribute to it the authority of moral judgment. He thus bore witness to a society in which rising numbers of people, disillusioned by science because they could not, in good conscience, participate in this idolatry but, lacking Weber's personal demon or any other moral commitment, resorted to avenues of salvation such as "the arms of the old churches [which were] opened widely and compassionately,"[6] and to gurus, cults, insanity, or suicide.

III. Continuity

The section you have just read sketches an approach to a history of sociology informed by the conception of sociology here developing. In this sketch I touch on one sociologist and his society, a society in the process of a colossal development or a colossal explication.

The fundamental characteristic of this kind of history of sociology is the commitment to a *good society*, and this characteristic is to me the essence of a *sociological* history of sociology. The two terms *commitment* and *good society* must be stressed, for together they establish that the central concept of this approach is that of a *normative* society, a term which entails an affective attitude and also supplies a criterion for judging societies, extant or past.

I have interpreted Weber as a critic of this society, bringing the experience of my own society to bear on my reading of him because I am eager to learn about the continuity between Weber's and mine — actually, two phases of the same society. This exercise in hermeneutics has been applied to a small part of a particular sociologist's work, but it is applicable as well to the study of any era in the history of sociology, to the field as a whole, to currents within it—indeed, to any human phenomenon. It implies a threefold continuity between who or what is to be interpreted—the interpretandum—and the interpreter. First, there is the conviction that the interpretandum's universe of discourse should be and can be translated into the interpreter's. Second, there is a quite different continuity: that of the remembrance or realization of sociology itself, of sociology that began with the central concept of a normative society which, inevitably, was accompanied by affect and supplied a criterion for assessing whatever given society, most cogently the individual sociologist's own: think of two such profoundly different thinkers as Auguste Comte and Karl Marx or, indeed, of most sociologists up to the early decades of this century, roughly up to Max Weber's proclamation of sociology as "value-free."

But at this time in our history the third continuity is even more important than these two; it is that which unites not only sociologists but all people of good will: inspiration by the idea of a good society can unite us for survival. For our time is marked by *dis*continuity, by the wholly new possibility of our and our planet's end. In regard to sociology in particular, there may be the hope that pointing to the continuities suggested is not whistling in the dark.

Notes

1. Max Weber, "Science as a Vocation" (1918, published 1919), in *From Max Weber: Essays in Sociology*, trans., ed., and introd. by H. H. Gerth and C. Wright Mills (New York: Oxford University Press, 1946), p. 135.
2. Ibid., pp. 154–5.
3. Ibid., p. 156.
4. Max Weber, "Politics as a Vocation" (1918, published 1919), in *From Max Weber*, p. 120.
5. Ibid., p. 127.
6. Weber, "Science as a Vocation," p. 155.

FOURTH ENTRY
SCHELER'S SHADOW ON US

Scheler's Shadow on Us

The characteristic of this history of sociology—commitment to a good society—is, of course, the commitment to an ideal, that is, something that can only be approached but never reached. The manifestations of such commitment by a given sociologist may be discerned in both advocacies and corresponding neglects found in the work of that sociologist. Thus, in the Max Weber of the preceding entry into our emerging sociology, there was the advocacy of *a genuine man*, a truly moral person, one who acts both responsibly and on principle. The clear implication of this advocacy is that a society composed of such genuine men is a good society. On the other hand, Weber neglects to explicate his conception of the two ethics that fuse in the genuine, truly moral person, missing the failure of the society in which he espoused his ideas to share his conviction of what constitutes a good man and a good society. Thus Weber didn't further explain these ideas or modify them on the basis of a truer assessment of his society. To articulate such a relation between a given sociologist and the surrounding society is an aim of this history of sociology.

Let us see how such a conception of the history of sociology—and of sociology—fares when applied to other sociologists—Max Scheler, Alfred Schutz, Karl Mannheim, Emile Durkheim.

I will begin with Scheler, examining his essay *Cognition and Work* (*Erkenntnis und Arbeit*, 1926 [See note 1]). Its subtitle, "A Study of the Value and the Limits of the Pragmatic *Motiv* ["*Motiv*" is both motive and motif] in the Cognition of the World" ("Eine Studie über Wert und Grenzen des pragmatischen Motivs in der Erkenntnis der Welt"), might make one expect Scheler will treat both the pragmatic motive in cognition and the pragmatic component of cognition; that is, one might expect him to engage in both a psychological and a phenomenological

inquiry. What he does instead is suggested—though *only* suggested—
by the following major subdivisions of his investigation: (1) the problem,
(2) essence and meanings of knowledge and cognition, and the kinds of
knowledge (each about ten pages long), (3) philosophic pragmatism
(about fifty pages), (4) methodological pragmatism (about twenty pages),
(5) on the philosophy of perception (the longest part, almost eighty
pages), (6) metaphysics of perception and the problem of reality (twenty
pages), and (7) an extremely brief conclusion from the point of view of
the sociology of knowledge (four pages). I will not follow this sequence,
which can hardly be called orderly or organic, and which I mention only
to give a vague idea of what Scheler discusses. Nor will I try to list, let
alone examine, all matters that come up for treatment, fleeting or in-
tensive, in this extraordinarily rich essay, which in its richness and
breathlessness is characteristic of Scheler.

Scheler begins his essay with this paragraph:

> The pathos modern man associates with the term "work" has become the
> more intensive the more he has struggled free of the spiritual traditions of
> antiquity and Christianity and sought to create for himself a view of the world
> and an ethos out of the conditions of his own existence and life. That pathos,
> which only found its sharpest expression in the words of the *Communist
> Manifesto* about work as the "only creator of all civilization and culture,"
> has not remained without a deep influence on the *philosophical conception
> of cognition*, even of the *essence of man* himself. The great intellectual move-
> ment of "pragmatism," in epistemology and metaphysics, is the best proof
> of this. Is man himself *homo rationalis* and not perhaps rather *homo faber*?
> This is the decisive question one has dared raise.[1]

If one were to proceed systematically, Scheler suggests, the problem
of the relation between cognition and work would have to be investigated
in five ways. There is, first, the historical and sociological approach,
which shows in detail how the cooperation of technology and science
has taken place and has developed. A second perspective is epistemological: its relevance has been shown by "pragmatic philosophy, from
James to Nietzsche, Bergson, and Vaihinger" (198); the epistemological
will be Scheler's own predominant perspective. Although he hardly deals
with it, the third deserves quotation because of its importance and because it shows Scheler's comprehensiveness of vision. "Our problem,"
he writes,

> further is a problem in *developmental physiology and psychology*, in more
> than one sense. That is to say, we must ask whether and in what degree
> there are relations of condition between the *instinctive* and *motor* behavior
> of the organism *and* the formation of the *images of the surrounding world*

(correspondingly in man, between regulated work and its forms and the forms of knowledge) and whether these relations lead to the formation of those physiological and psychic organs and functions which at any point are necessary to enlarge the world image in various respects of, e.g., the activity of sense and memory. That is, we must ask this question differentially in regard to the complex direction in which the living in general unfolds, in regard to the psychic abilities of different kinds of animals in relation to one another and in relation to man, in regard to the direction of the development of knowledge of primitive man toward the civilized man of culture, in regard to the unfolding from child to adult, and finally in regard to the development of knowledge of historical man. (199)

In the fourth approach the relation between cognition and work can be illuminated by studying the physiology and psychology of work, including such pathological cases as amnesia and visual amnesia; and finally, there is the pedagogic application of the problem which is pertinent, for instance, to the discussion of vocational versus liberal arts education.

Central among the mistakes of pragmatism is to take one kind of knowledge for knowledge as such. Pragmatism does not recognize that knowledge is a relation of being, an existential relation, which must not be defined in terms presupposing "knowledge"—more specifically, that it is "the relation of *participation* of a being [*Seienden*] in the specific existence [*Sosein*] of another being without involving any change whatever in that existence" (203; see also 227, 251). Being participation, Scheler argues, knowledge cannot serve knowledge but only some becoming, a becoming different; and depending on the aim of becoming, we have three kinds of knowledge. They serve (1) the becoming of the person who knows: "formational knowledge" [*Bildungswissen*]; (2) "the becoming of the *world* and (perhaps) the atemporal ground of its supreme existence and being itself . . . let this knowledge for the sake of the godhead be called *redemptive knowledge* [*Erlösungswissen*]" (205); and (3) "the becoming of the practical domination and transformation of the world for our human goals and purposes . . . the knowledge of positive 'science,' the 'knowledge of domination' or achievement [*Herrschafts- oder Leistungswissen*]," the only one that pragmatism is concerned with (205). Not only, however, are there the other kinds of knowledge, they also are hierarchically ordered: redemptive knowledge is supreme, formational knowledge follows, and the knowledge of domination is lowest (205).[2]

But not only does pragmatism "falsify the idea of knowledge," it also ignores "the fundamental distinction" between "knowledge of essence ["essential knowledge," *Wesenswissen*] and knowledge of contingent facts," or between a priori and a posteriori knowledge (232). The two kinds are mediated by what Scheler calls *functionalization* (198, 232), a concept that he developed a few years before in *On the Eternal in Man* (1921), and that Manfred S. Frings quotes in his very worthwhile introduction to a new edition of *Erkenntnis und Arbeit*.[3] It is important enough for an understanding of this essay that I quote Scheler at length:

> Essential knowledge is functionalized into a law concerning the mere "application": of the intellect to contingent facts that grasps, analyzes, looks at, judges the world of contingent facts as "determined" "according to" essential connections. . . . For instance, when we conclude *according to* a principle without concluding *from* it, obey an aesthetic rule . . . without in the remotest sense having it in our minds in the mode of a formulated proposition, essential insights come "into function" without becoming explicitly visible to the mind. Only in the experience of incorrectness, of deviation from a law, which we do not for all that have consciously in mind as a law, does it dawn on us that we have been led by an insight, as also . . . happens in all stirrings of conscience, which more nearly raise a protest against what is false than . . . pointing to the good; but behind them, nevertheless, there stands a *positive* insight into the good and into a positive ideal of our individual and general human life. As essential insights are thus "functionalized," a *kind of true growth of the human spirit*, both in individual life and in the course of history, occurs . . . which is *essentially different* from all aptitudes acquired or . . . inherited by influences on the human organism and its sensory zones, as well as from all genesis that is understandable in merely psychological terms. . . . A becoming and growing of reason itself, that is, of its stock of *a priori* laws of selection and function, becomes understandable through this functionalization of essential insight.[4]

This "functionalization" appears hardly more operational than Hegel's cunning of reason. And Scheler's devotion to essential knowledge, redemptive or formational or metaphysical, has a strong emotional component. For instance:

> [Pragmatism] renounces not only all essential knowledge of *absolute reality*, that is, metaphysical and religious knowledge. For it is certain that absolute reality, if changeable at all, can be changed only *by itself* [unlike the world which pragmatic knowledge aims at changing]. . . . Only insofar as personality itself were a function of the divine spirit could the divine spirit change by means of it, that is, change itself by means of it, e.g., grow or redeem itself—provided it needed redemption.[5]

This suggests a longing for grace—as a passage from *Problems of a Sociology of Knowledge* suggests a longing for absolute knowledge in the midst of relativism—but *this* passage has an unexpected effect: "We escape relativism [Scheler writes] . . . by hanging up, as it were, the sphere of absolute ideas and values, which corresponds to the essential idea of man, enormously [*ganz gewaltig*] much higher above all actual hitherto existing historical value systems. . . ."[6] Scheler *hangs* the *logos*, and literally "violently much higher" (even though "violently," a term often used by Scheler, is colloquial for "enormous" or "mighty"), thus saving it from relativization.[7] As in the preceding passage he preserved absolute reality from external change, he here preserves the spirit by moving it out of reach, but "hanging" and "violently much higher" suggest salvation or redemption by killing—liberate Vietnamese villages by destruction. Scheler's mood is still ours or among us; he even was ahead of his time, perhaps.

But such unheeding passion for the absolute, emotional, and cognitive is only one of Scheler's relations to it. Another is suggested by his claim that only knowledge of essences "is the first and immediate bearer of the predicate *'evident,'* "[8] and *this* recalls Georg Simmel's convinced, serene, even ironic claim that "all that can be proved can also be disputed. Only the unprovable is indisputable."[9] Scheler's own faith thus finds expression not only in his taxonomy of kinds of knowledge (and on many other occasions) but also in such evidences of his own knowledge of it, hence of his own conviction, as his claim that while work acquaints us with the "contingent objective world of images[10] and their laws," man also has a very different possibility of knowing, namely, "the philosophic," which suspends "the practical attitude" and "tears itself loose from" contingency in order to look in two other directions. One "is the realm of essences, that is, the primordial phenomena and ideas of which the images are only 'instances' . . . ; the other is the stream of drives, impulses, forces which merely manifest themselves in these 'images.' " Scheler continues:

> It is not "work" at the world which leads to such cognitive possibilities. What leads to the first is wonderment, humility, and spiritual love of what is essential, [and such knowledge is] gained by a phenomenological reduction of what there is. What leads to the second is a Dionysian abandonment in feeling-at-one and becoming-one with the impulse part of which is also all our craving, wishing and urging.

> Only in the greatest tension between these two attitudes and only in overcoming this tension in the unity of the person is proper philosophic cognition born.[11]

Here, then, *in nuce* is Scheler's "philosophical anthropology,"[12] his conception of personality, and at the same time his self-portrait. He is one, as he writes elsewhere,[13] who goes into rhapsodies, and who longs to do right by both his mind and his instincts.[14] With such conviction of the possibility or at least the undeniable challenge of essential knowledge (and of redemptive knowledge), Scheler can admit, as it were, now hypothetically, now with certainty, that the essence of reality itself is resistance. Hypothetically:

> . . . if the investigation of this question [of the essence of "reality"] were to show that being real itself is given originarily only in the resistance with which some inner and outer configurations of things assert themselves against the impulses (of instinct and will) of striving . . . then the pragmatically conditioned knowledge of nature would be securely founded in a primordial phenomenon of the world's ontic structure itself.[15]

With certainty Scheler asserts:

> Imagine the whole content of the natural world view[16] dismantled piece by piece, let all colors pale, all sounds fade away, the sphere of body consciousness disappear with all its content, the form of space and time and all forms of being (categories) of things level off into an indeterminate existence [*Dasein*]—then there remains as that which cannot be dismantled a simple, no longer analyzable impression of reality as such: the impression of something simply "resisting" the spontaneous activity. . . . Being real is not being object . . . rather it is being resistance against the primordially flowing spontaneity that is one and the same in will and attention of every kind.[17]

Reality being based on resistance and thus consciousness-transcendent, it is "work on the world," not contemplation, that is "the essential root of all positive science, all induction, all experiment" (363), and its theory also is the foundation of "pure and in the distinct sense philosophic knowledge" (282). But we must remember all three kinds of knowledge; for Scheler, it is the task of the sociology of knowledge to explore relations between them and social characteristics and structures.[18] In the present essay, however, his perspective is more nearly historical and diagnostic. Scheler points out that hitherto the great cultures have developed the kinds of knowledge one-sidedly ("India, redemptive knowledge . . . ; China and Greece, formational knowledge; the West since the beginning of the twelfth century, the work knowledge [*Arbeitswissen*] of the positive social sciences": 210). Now, however, Scheler argues,

> the world hour has come when an equalization and at the same time a complementation of the one-sided directions of the spirit must be prepared. The future of the history of human culture will stand under the sign of this equalization and complementation—not under the sign of a one-sided rejection of one kind of knowledge at the expense of another nor of an exclusive cultivation of what has historically been "characteristic" of each culture area.

And while the torch of science originally lit in Greece will not be extinguished by any romanticism, whether Christian or Indian, science is not enough for man.

> Indeed, even with the ideal perfection of this positive-technical process, man as a spiritual being could remain absolutely empty—he could sink back into a barbarism in comparison with which all so-called nature peoples would be true Athenian Greeks. Indeed, since all work knowledge . . . must in the last analysis serve formational knowledge . . . the barbarism with a scientific-systematic foundation would even be the most terrible of all imaginable barbarisms. But in its turn . . . formational knowledge . . . must subordinate itself to the idea of redemptive knowledge and has its ultimate purpose in serving it. For in the last analysis, all knowledge is of the godhead and for the godhead.[19]

As we have heard, the technique of obtaining essential knowledge is the phenomenological reduction, but Scheler modifies Husserl by arguing that it

> requires not only the switching off of the acts that give the element of reality: it requires, at the same time, the switching on of that disinterested [begier-defrei] love for the being and the being-worthy of all things which replaces the relation of domination by a new, spiritual relation to the world (*amor intellectualis*). At the same time, it requires a transition of a technical nature, physically and spiritually, of the energy of activity that was anchored in the dominating relation to nature . . . to that of love for nature, that is, to the supreme condition of every purely objective behavior altogether that is given over to the object itself—in the first place, of "purely" theoretical behavior.[20]"

To conclude, what I have said does not do justice to Scheler's mind at work in this essay, which is very fast and concise and at the same time loose, surprising, puzzling, in short, difficult. Scheler is much less discursive than the orderly arrangement of lines suggests; he is more like a torrent, and one that changes directions all the time; he makes trouble for the commentator. Let me try something much more modest than doing him justice: I'll give a quick historical glance and close with a sociological observation.

Nineteen hundred and seventy-eight, the semicentennial of Scheler's death, was the centennial of Charles Sanders Peirce's essay, "How to Make Our Ideas Clear."[21] It was in this essay, Scheler tells us,[22] that, according to William James, pragmatism was introduced into philosophy. It was the time of a first taking stock of industrialization and capitalism which, almost half a century later when Scheler wrote *his* essay, had significantly spread to Germany and developed generally; it also was the time after World War I, the time of *The Three-Penny Opera* and *The Blue Angel*. Scheler made the effort to revive kinds of knowledge that had come to occupy questionable places. He recognized the transhistorical and transcultural importance of pragmatic knowledge, anchored as it is in man's relation to his surrounding. The tension between that effort and this recognition is far more widely felt today, another half century later, than it was then, for in the meantime we have had, among many other things, the *Bulletin of the Atomic Scientists* in response to nuclear science, above all the nuclear bomb, the threatening exhaustion of natural resources, including air and water, and, possibly more important as an agent of change and possibly as a promise, the as yet unforeseeable position of the West which in the disproportionate importance it has given to the cultivation and practice of the knowledge of domination also has perfected the art of digging its own grave. Scheler saw this long before most of us did, and his warning, passionate and passionately intelligent, can still be heeded now—and must be, far more preemptorily than when he sounded it.

Notes

1. Max Scheler, "Erkenntnis und Arbeit," in *Die Wissensformen und die Gesellschaft* (1926), in *Gesammelte Werke*, 2d rev. ed., with addenda, ed. Maria Scheler (Berne: Francke, 1960), vol. VIII, p. 193. It is puzzling that Scheler, let alone this work, should not even be mentioned in Hannah Arendt's *The Human Condition* (Chicago: University of Chicago Press, 1958), which is so intimately related in its topic.
2. Elsewhere Scheler derives three kinds of knowledge by the criterion not of aim of becoming, but of origin: the desire of saving one's being leads to religious knowledge; wonderment leads to metaphysical knowledge; and the wish to act in the world and to control it leads to positive knowledge: Max Scheler, "Probleme einer Soziologie des Wissens" (1924)—the first essay in *Die Wissensformen und die Gesellschaft*, in which *Cognition and Work* is the second—pp. 65–6; cf. translation of the first part of this essay, "Formal Problems" (of the sociology of knowledge), pp. 52–69, by Rainer Koehne in *The Sociology of Knowledge: A Reader*, ed. by James E. Curtis and John W. Petras (New York: Praeger, 1970), as "The Sociology of Knowledge: Formal Problems," pp. 170–86, at pp. 180–1, and the translation of the whole essay by Manfred S. Frings, as *Problems of a Sociology of Knowledge*, ed. and introd. by Kenneth W. Stikkers (London, Boston and Henley: Routledge & Kegan Paul, 1980); see pp. 77–8. The most explicit Scheler comes to addressing the relation between the two triads of knowledge is to treat them as synonymous: "religious, metaphysical, and positive knowledge, or, as we can also say, knowledge of salvation or of redemption, knowledge of culture, and practical knowledge, or knowledge for control of nature" in *Problems of a Sociology of Knowledge*, p. 44.
3. Manfred S. Frings, "Einleitung des Herausgebers," pp. vii–xxi (esp. xv–xvi), in *Erkenntnis und Arbeit*, ed. by Max Scheler (Frankfurt: Klostermann, 1977).

4. Max Scheler, *Vom Ewigen im Menschen*, vol. 1, *Religiöse Erneuerung* (Leipzig: Der Neue Geist, 1921) ("Probleme der Religion [Zur religiösen Erneuerung]") (1918?) ("II. Die Wesensphänomenologie der Religion, 4. Wachstum und Abnahme der natürlichen Gotteserkenntnis"), pp. 445–7 (some italicizations omitted); cf. Max Scheler, *On the Eternal in Man*, trans. by Bernard Noble, (from *Gesammelte Werke*, vol. V, 4th ed. [Berne: Francke, 1954]) (New York: Harper, 1960), pp. 201–2.

5. Scheler, *Erkenntnis und Arbeit*, p. 233.

6. Scheler, *Probleme einer Soziologie des Wissens*, p. 26. Cf. *Problems of a Sociology of Knowledge*, pp. 41–2.

7. My thanks to Rainer E. Koehne for calling my attention, many years ago, to this pun of "gewaltig."

8. Scheler, *Erkenntnis und Arbeit*, p. 231.

9. Georg Simmel, "Aus dem nachgelassenen Tagebuche" (*Logos* 8 [1919–1920]: 121–51), reprinted in *Fragmente und Aufsätze aus dem Nachlass und Veröffentlichungen der letzten Jahre*, ed. Gertrud Kantorowicz (München: Drei Masken Verlag, 1923), p. 4, quoted in *The Sociology of Georg Simmel*, trans., ed., and introd. by Kurt H. Wolff (Glencoe, Ill,: Free Press, 1950), p. xx.

10. On "images," see Scheler, *Erkenntnis und Arbeit*, p. 287.

11. Ibid., p. 362 (italics omitted).

12. He often refers to his forthcoming, central work on philosophical anthropology but did not complete it beyond the sketch, published in the year of his death, *Man's Place in Nature* (1928), trans. and introd. by Hans Meyerhoff (1961) (New York: Noonday, 1962). Cf. Hans-Georg Gadamer, "Max Scheler—der Verschwender" (1974), in *Max Scheler im Gegenwartsgeschehen der Philosophie*, ed. Paul Good (Berne: Francke, 1977), pp. 11–18, esp. 17–18. (Much else in this volume is worth reading.)

13. As he writes in regard to his *Probleme einer Soziologie des Wissens*, p. 17; *Problems of a Sociology of Knowledge*, p. 33.

14. "Functionalized" (?) into his theory of "real" and "ideal factors," his (not original) distinction between *Realsoziologie* (roughly, sociology of the real factors) and *Kultursoziologie* (sociology of culture, of ideal factors), and his association of the requirement of a theory of human drives with the former and of a theory of the human mind with the latter. Cf. ibid., esp. pp. 18–23; *Problems of a Sociology of Knowledge*, pp. 36–40.

15. Scheler, *Erkenntnis und Arbeit*, p. 281 (italics omitted).

16. "The absolutely natural world view . . . is a . . . historically-sociologically unchangeable 'constant' which . . . can be ascertained by a (difficult) peeling off of the 'authentic' and 'live' traditions which in every concrete world view of a group are always interwoven with it" (Max Scheler, "Weltanschauungslehre, Soziologie und Weltanschauungssetzung" (1922), in *Schriften zur Soziologie und Weltanschauungslehre*, vol. 1, Moralia (Leipzig: Der Neue Geist Verlag, 1923), p. 5 (italics omitted). A year later, Scheler had dropped this concept and replaced it by that of the "relative natural world view," which refers to the sum total of what is taken for granted by a given group: *Probleme einer Soziologie des Wissens*, pp. 60–3; *Problems of a Sociology of Knowledge*, pp. 74–6.

17. Scheler, *Erkenntnis und Arbeit*, p. 363 (italics omitted).

18. Cf. *Probleme einer Soziologie des Wissens*, pp. 69–190; *Problems of a Sociology of Knowledge*, pp. 81–182.

19. *Erkenntnis und Arbeit*, p. 211, (italics omitted). Cf. Max Weber, 1904–1905 (quoted in first entry above): " 'Specialists without spirit, sensualists without heart; this nullity imagines that it has attained a level of civilization never before achieved' " (*The Protestant Ethic and the Spirit of Capitalism*, trans. Talcott Parsons, New York: Scribner, 1930, p. 182). It is impossible to imagine that Scheler was not familiar with this passage.

20. Scheler, *Erkenntnis und Arbeit*, p. 282. Related to this general view of science, philosophy and their state in Scheler's—and largely our—time is Scheler's more particular critique of "value-free science" and Max Weber's view of it. Cf. "Weltanschauungslehre, Soziologie und Weltanschauungssetzung," pp. 11, 12, 17; "Max Webers Ausschaltung, der Philosophie (Zur Psychologie und Soziologie der nominalistischen Denkart)" (1921 or 1922), in *Die Wissensformen und die Gesellschaft*, pp. 430–38, and Maria Scheler, "Nachwort der Herausgeberin," ibid., p. 481. On Scheler's critique of modern science, see William Leiss, *The Domination of Nature* (New York: Braziller, 1972), p. 88, and chap. 5, "Science and Domination," esp. (on Scheler) pp. 103–19.

21. *Popular Science Monthly*, January 1878.

22. Scheler, *Erkenntnis und Arbeit*, pp. 212.

FIFTH ENTRY
INTO ALFRED SCHUTZ'S WORLD

Into Alfred Schutz's World

Like Max Weber, Scheler tries to put science in its place. Weber insisted that science cannot tell us how to live; Scheler, at least by implication, resorts to the "knowledge of essense" to tell us. Weber's understanding of science appears more just; Scheler's more polemical. Both warn against blind trust in science, but Scheler with far more confidence in religion than Weber has. It is abundantly clear that both were worried about their time, their society, yet neither seems to have taken "the decline of the West" seriously, although they knew the work of this title, as well as its author, Oswald Spengler. Yet in their critiques of Spengler's "dilettantism" they missed the thrust the title proclaims.[1] Scheler, however, six years after Weber's death (1920), only eight years after Weber's speeches on science and on politics, clearly showed his alertness to "fascist and communist" *Bünde* who no longer seek truth and justice ("Ideas" they despise) but a "*Herrn*" (lord, master—*Führer* will soon turn out to be the word) who would tell them what they must do and not do. And Scheler cites the concluding remarks of the second volume of Spengler's *Der Untergang des Abendlandes*,[2] in which Spengler ends his long work with a prediction of caesarism that must follow the present time with its idolatry of money.

In advocating essence-knowledge Scheler neglects the danger of its gliding into obscurantism, fanaticism, and sectarianism, including fascism, bolshevism, and nazism. We have seen the limits of Max Weber's far greater political realism and above all far greater political engagement; and we have seen Scheler's corresponding neglect of what it takes to bring about a good society; his commitment to society was far weaker than Weber's.

Let us now examine Alfred Schutz, who knew Scheler's work well and wrote about it.[3] But we want to try reading Schutz in his own terms, entering his world.

The title of this entry into our emerging sociology tells its intent: to enter the world of Alfred Schutz himself, rather than "Alfred Schutz's work," because I wish to do right by something that is as trivial as it is important, as obvious as it is quite generally ignored, namely that works, even in philosophy, not to mention sociology, are written by human beings (hard as it may sometimes be to believe). Taking this seriously means that there is a point in the effort to understand a piece of writing (or any other work) at which we must go outside of it and to its author so that our understanding may be illuminated by encountering the human being the author is, which includes the time and place in which the author lived, just as in this same process author, time, and place are illuminated by illuminating the work.

I. On Schutz's Concept of "World"

"World"—as in the "world" of history or the "world" of Alfred Schutz or the "world" of Alfred Schutz's work—is an important element in Schutz's conceptual inventory. But in Schutz's conceptual inventory, there is, as far as I know, none of the three worlds I have just made use of—the worlds of history, of author, of an author's like Schutz's work. I think my effort to enter Schutz's world through his work (more realistically and modestly, part of his work) tests his concept of world itself.

The locus classicus of Schutz's discussion of "world"—William James's "sub-universe"—is his paper "On Multiple Realities."[4] In this seminal paper, Schutz identifies "world" or "sub-universe" or, as he prefers to call it, "finite province of meaning," by its "cognitive style." The cognitive style of a world has six "basic characteristics": (1) "a specific tension of consciousness," (2) "a specific *epoché*," (3) "a prevalent form of spontaneity," (4) "a specific form of experiencing oneself," (5) "a specific form of sociality," and (6) "a specific time perspective."[5]

In my effort to get into Alfred Schutz's own world, I find it noteworthy that a world is defined by its cognitive style. But as Brenda Powell has shown, there is in Schutz also another approach to "world," which she found in Schutz's posthumous *Reflections on the Problem of Relevance*.[6] Here, "world" is not something to be identified by its cognitive style but something constituted in terms of relevance. Nevertheless, Powell comes to the conclusion that "the actor in both [approaches to "world"] 'treats' . . . his worlds as intellectual Projects."[7] As we shall see (in section V), this may not be so. But the nature of Schutz's concept of "world" raises a question that is another marker on my way to Alfred Schutz's own world. Now, however, we are leaving the matter of this concept "world." In departing, we observe that among the worlds Schutz treats there are those of everyday life, of scientific theory, and, more cursorily, of phantasms and dreams. But there is none of history, none of social criticism, none of writing in philosophy or other humanities or social science, or of the author of such writing, let alone of the relation between these last two worlds, on which, as I said, I wish to focus. And we want to remember Schutz's two approaches to the problem of world by cognitive style and by relevance and Powell's claim that in both the actor's worlds figure as intellectual projects.

II. Intersubjective Understanding

We now come to another "important element in Schutz's conceptual inventory," intersubjective understanding or, more precisely, the nature of my knowledge of another human being. Schutz's motive for pursuing the problem of intersubjective understanding, it appears, is to show "Husserl's Importance for the Social Sciences,"[8] to quote the formulation Schutz used as the title of one of his papers; more generally, it is to show the relevance of phenomenology to sociology in particular.

In this undertaking, his point of departure is a basic concept of Max Weber's sociology, that of "subjectively intended meaning" or, more briefly, "subjective meaning." "Subjective meaning" refers to whatever "goes on," intellectually and emotionally, in an individual who produces something—anything—a sentence, a cry, a building, a string quartet. It refers to what the individual means by this producing. "Subjective meaning" contrasts with "objective meaning," which is what that individual's producing means to me who wants to understand it, irrespective of what it means to the producer, irrespective of its subjective meaning.[9] The subjective meaning, of course, is the aim of understanding in the social sciences and humanities, the hoped-for result of acting on the injunction to get inside the other, to place oneself in another's shoes, to look at the world from another's point of view. This injunction espouses what may be called methodological relativism (in contrast to epistemological and moral relativism), the view that the relative and unique in human life does not contradict the absolute and universal in human life. And it may be worth noting that the demand to try understanding the other in its own terms—whatever the other may be, an individual, artifact, culture, or historical period—is a variant of Husserl's demand, "to the things themselves."

In his analysis of understanding others, Schutz distinguishes four kinds or types of others: those in my physical presence (who live in my *Umwelt*): my consociates; those who live at the same time as I but elsewhere (who live in my *Mitwelt*): my contemporaries; those who lived before me (in my *Vorwelt*): my predecessors; and those who will live after me (in my *Nachwelt*): my successors.[10] This apparently so plausible typology raises serious problems, but I can comment on only one, which is the most pertinent marker on my way into Alfred Schutz's world. This problem results from what Schutz says and fails to say about the possibility of my access to the subjective meanings of the four types. Briefly: I can get at the subjective meaning of contemporaries and predecessors only by means of typification (and by definition not at all at that of successors since I cannot know them); but Schutz's discussion of the "genuine understanding of the other"[11] leaves it unclear whether I can attain direct, rather than typified or typical understanding of my consociate.

Schutz argues convincingly that to understand contemporaries and predecessors, typification is inescapable. He shows the extraordinary variability in the articulation or concretization of the type I construct without giving it much, if any, thought in my everyday interaction with others. Concreteness, for instance, decreases conspicuously in the following series: my letter carrier, *a* letter carrier, postal employees, post office, an institution.[12]

A moment's reflection shows that within Schutz's conceptual inventory, my understanding of my consociate, my "genuine understanding of the other," of you who are sitting right by me and, furthermore, whom I know as thoroughly as I know anybody, cannot be anything but typical either, though my understanding of you is incomparably more subtle than my understanding even of my letter carrier (if that is all he or she is). Nor is it difficult to understand the reason for this sometimes sad, sometimes fortunate circumstance: you and I are not the *same* individual; "*perfect* cognition presupposes perfect identity."[13] We have different biographies, even if we were identical twins, and if only because the world that I see looks different from the world that you see, beginning with the most literal sense, that you and I cannot be at the same place at the same time, for each of us also is a body, which fills space, and by the time we exchange places (recognizing and acting on Schutz's "reciprocity of perspectives"),[14] each of us has changed, if for no other reason, again, than because we also are bodies.[15] Schutz does stress the never more than asymptotic character of intersubjective understanding, but his conception of subjective meaning seems at least not to rule out the possibility of its being "genuine," rather than only typical and thus approximate. As far as I know, Schutz does not explicitly confront the question of whether such understanding is possible, and if it is, how.

There thus appears to be a discrepancy in his conceptual structure, which demands accounting for.

III. Schutz's Social Scientist

Schutz's conception of the social scientist can give us a clue.[16] The social scientist has no relations with his fellowmen, but only observes and tries to understand them as types (Max Weber's "ideal types"); he observes them against his typology and tests his typology against his observations. In other words, the social scientist does what we all do in the mundane world. But in the mundane world, the kind and degree of our typifying depend on our purposes and interests—the very purposes and interests that Schutz's social scientist must suspend. It follows that the other, in both the mundane and the scientific world, can be understood only typically. How then can Schutz speak of grasping another's subjective meaning, of the "genuine understanding of the other," without at the same time warning us against any expectation, any hope that we can grasp subjective meaning other than typically and thus that "genuine understanding of the other" is a misleading designation? Is there an alternative in my access to the other—my consociate, contemporary, predecessor—that would make possible the actual, genuine, rather than only typical and approximate understanding of subjective meaning? Can Schutz's discrepancy be clarified by reference to an unacknowledged but perhaps hoped-for access to the other behind, as it were, his explicit one?

IV. Schutz and Husserl

Here it helps to go back to Husserl, who is so important for understanding Schutz's approach. The fifth of Husserl's *Cartesian Meditations* presents an extraordinarily careful analysis of the process of "constituting" the other by "appresentation," a "passive synthesis" by which, in Schutz's formulation,

> an actual experience refers back to another experience which is not given in actuality. . . . In other words, the appresented does not attain an actual presence.[17]

Yet there is, for Husserl, an objective world, and "the first form of objectivity" is "intersubjective nature":

The first things constituted in the form of community and the foundation of all other intersubjective common things is the commonness of nature, along with that of the other's body and psycho-physical ego.[18]

In his lucid and helpful "very condensed account of Husserl's fifth Meditation," Schutz agrees with Sartre that Husserl

has shown in a masterful way how in the mundane sphere man and fellow-man are compossible and coexistent, how within this sphere the Other becomes manifest, how within it concordant behavior, communication, etc., occur. Yet he has not shown the possibility of a coexisting transcendental Alter Ego constituted within and by the activities of the transcendental ego. This, however, would be necessary in order to overcome the solipsistic argument in the transcendental sphere.[19]

To glean a pertinent comment on Husserl and intersubjectivity we consider the following passage from the first paragraph of the Preface to Merleau-Ponty's *Phenomenology of Perception:*

Phenomenology is the study of essences, and according to it, all problems amount to finding definitions of essences—the essence of perception or the essence of consciousness, for instance. But phenomenology also is a philosophy which puts essences back into existence and does not expect that one can understand the human being and the world otherwise than by starting with their "facticity." It is a transcendental philosophy which, the better to understand the affirmations coming out of the natural attitude places them in abeyance; but it also is a philosophy for which the world always is "already there," prior to reflection as an inalienable presence; a philosophy whose entire effort is to find again this naive contact with the world in order finally to give it a philosophical status.[20]

According to Schutz (and Sartre), Husserl has failed to establish intersubjectivity as intersubjectivity among transcendental egos or subjects, but this means that he has failed to provide theoretical grounding for sociality, hence society, hence the study of society. And according to Merleau-Ponty, Husserl is looking for essences in what for this purpose he must bracket, that is, existence, which thus turns out to be the source of both insight and obfuscation. But existence, which means existence in the world of everyday life, Schutz's "paramount reality," is all that we have to take our departure from on our way to essences; the "world," or our culture, or our received notions, is all there is for us to suspend. It guides us in an ever tentative manner, which is where the element of obfuscation comes in. But this tentative manner is there for us to suspend, and this is where insight or clarification comes in.

The problem, it would appear, lies in Merleau-Ponty's observation that for Husserl "the world always is 'already there' prior to reflection." We saw this in the Husserl quotation on "the commonness of nature," "intersubjective" nature, but the only conclusion Husserl allows himself to draw from the world's thereness is that we must bracket it; the only response to the world is that it is that which invites us to seek its *eidos*. In other words, his interest in the world is *epistemological*. For we can respond cognitively to the world also as having moral, aesthetic, or political meaning, and such a response may also lead to action. But for Husserl, there *is* the world, there *is* the other, there *are* others; yet it seems as if he were not confident enough, did not trust world and other and others enough not to have to put all his effort into trying to *constitute* them phenomenologically—to be sure, in order to ground rational praxis (and "to be sure" in two quite different senses: *indeed* and [for Husserl] *to be certain*). Husserl failed to ground transcendental intersubjectivity theoretically because of his selective, fragmentary, namely, epistemological approach to the world and human beings.[21]

V. Schutz's Conflict

Let us return to Alfred Schutz. If it is true—even to the extent that it is true—that in the theory of both Husserl and Schutz, the world and fellow human beings have exclusively epistemological meaning and appeal, we may want to ask why this should be so. In asking this, our position is no longer within their work but outside of it, on the way *to* the authors and their place and time. We surmise a characteristic of these authors, namely, an ascetic attitude toward relations among people—the kind of asceticism that is also evident in Max Weber's conception of "value-free" social science. But the discrepancy we suspected in Schutz suggests that this asceticism, this distrust of any role of feeling as ground of a rational praxis, has a competitor, that it militates against another attitude toward the world. This is his desire for the "genuine" understanding of fellowmen, a longing, perhaps, to attenuate the asceticism, a desire to do more justice to feeling.

Indeed, it seems that there are some other features of Schutz's work than the discrepancy I mentioned that make me suspect there is conflict between these two components. There are two theoretically unassimilated elements that nevertheless make their appearance often in Schutz's writing, namely, "the fundamental anxiety" of "the basic experience of each of us: I know that I shall die and I fear to die,"[22] and the "growing older together" in the "we-relation".[23] In both cases, who is talking or when are among the questions that go wholly unexamined. That longing and desire might also be traceable in such of Schutz's papers as "Making

Music Together" (1951), "Mozart and the Philosophers" (1956),[24] the early "Thou-Problem" ("Das Duproblem" [1924–28]),[25] or "Tiresias, or Our Knowledge of Future Events" (1959),[26] and possibly, too, in his later interests in the *Lebenswelt*[27] and in relevance, so that Powell's claim that even the world constituted in terms of relevance is an intellectual project for its constitutor may need qualification.

As Max Weber was eminently political, Schutz was eminently musical, but both found it necessary and even decent and orderly, and morally responsible, to keep these passionate interests from entering their conceptions of social science, and indeed, in Schutz's case, his conception of philosophy as a whole. (This did not prevent them from making these interests, provided they found them in other individuals or periods, objects of scientific investigation.) Weber's *Wertfreiheit*, his prohibition to pass value judgments—which Schutz, incidentally, took over unanalyzed—would thus parallel Schutz's prohibiting social scientists to enter into relations with the human beings they study. The very term "puppet," which Schutz uses as a synonym of "ideal type,"[28] reminds us that the type should not be taken as anything like a simplified description of an actual individual. But the term also reflects the abstinence to be striven for by the sociologist from any but an epistemological interest in his fellowman.[29]

VI. Two Questions

My concluding remarks must be limited to the recording, for future analysis, of two questions that have come up.

First, I said in the beginning that my effort to get into Alfred Schutz's world tests his concept of world itself. I suggest that what is involved in this paper is an empirical test. We found two features of Schutz's work in particular that served as markers "on our way to his world": the consistently epistemological constitution of "world" and the discrepancy in the conception of understanding my consociate. Since we could discover no solution to the questions raised by these two features within Schutz's writing, we went outside of it to its author. In this way, or better, *on* this way, the author and his world emerged at the same time. On the one hand, there is a human being in unresolved conflict between monopolization by an epistemological concern and the longing to overcome this monopolization by accepting and drawing theoretical consequences from his aesthetic and moral needs which in the theory presented by him are suppressed. On the other hand, the society of this human being is one in which such conflict is widespread and finds many expressions—between science and religion, technology and art, manipulation and love, and many more.

What is the relation between this, admittedly extremely sketchy, approach to "world" and Schutz's analysis of "world"? It might be useful to begin tackling this question by examining the ways in which Schutz's six "basic characteristics" of the "cognitive style" of a world and the several relevances he discusses figure in the present exploration, and more specifically, by asking how time and place are "illuminated by illuminating the work," as I also claimed. Must something be modified in my procedure or be added to Schutz's conceptual inventory to allow time and place to figure in it?

Second, in summarizing Schutz's fourfold typology of others (consociates, contemporaries, predecessors, successors), I mentioned that though plausible, it raises serious problems, but that for our purposes only one typology could be commented on, that of understanding my consociate. I will mention one other, and only for reasons of methodology. My friend with whom I am talking in my room is, by Schutz's definition, my consociate. But the moment he closes the door behind him, he turns into my contemporary, as if our friendship and all the memories attached to it, our mutual affection, played a secondary role compared to the difference between physical copresence and physical separateness. Of course, there is a difference between somebody physically being with me and physically not being with me, but what Schutz's scheme leaves unexplored is precisely the nature of this difference. I suggest that a way to find out is by the most painstaking observation of myself in relation to my friend as he is getting up from his chair, goes toward the door, opens it, goes through it, and leaves me alone with the sound of his footsteps until even this sound disappears. This empirical method parallels that of the present paper, and I imagine that if one were to apply it, modifications in the description of the consociate, contemporary, and differences between them would result[30]—just as a careful examination of the first of my concluding questions, that of "world," is likely to entail a modification of that concept and of what it tries to grasp.

Notes

1. Cf. H. H. Gerth and C. Wright Mills, "Introduction: The Man and His Work," in *From Max Weber: Essays in Sociology*, trans., ed., and introd. by Gerth and Mills (New York: Oxford University Press, 1946), p. 70; Marianne Weber, *Max Weber: A Biography* (1926), trans. and ed. by Harry Zohn (New York, London, Sydney, Toronto: Wiley, 1975), pp. 674–5.

2. Cf. Scheler, *Probleme einer Soziologie des Wissens* in *Die Wissensformen und die Gesellsschaft*, (see n. 1 in previous entry), p. 183; *Problems of a Sociology of Knowledge*, (see n. 2 in previous entry), p. 180 and n. 177.

3. Above all, "Scheler's Theory of Intersubjectivity and the General Thesis of the Alter Ego" (1942), in Alfred Schutz, *Collected Papers*, vol. I, ed. and introd. by Maurice Natanson (The Hague: Nijhoff, 1962), pp. 150–79 (henceforth CP I); "Max Scheler's Philosophy" (1956) and "Max Scheler's Epistemology and Ethics" (1957–58), in Alfred Schutz, *Collected Papers*, vol. III, ed. by Ilse Schutz, and introd. by Aron Gurwitsch (The Hague: Nijhoff, 1966), pp. 133–44, 145–78. On Scheler's significance for Schutz, see Helmut R. Wagner, *Alfred Schutz: An Intellectual Biography* (Chicago: University of Chicago Press, 1983), *passim*; consult Topical Index and Index of Names.

4. Alfred Schutz, "On Multiple Realities" (1945), CP I, pp. 207–59, esp. 207; also see "Don Quixote and the Problem of Reality" (1954), in *Collected Papers*, vol. II, ed. and introd. by Arvid Brodersen (The Hague: Nijhoff, 1964), p. 135 (henceforth CP II).

5. Schutz, "On Multiple Realities," p. 230.

6. Alfred Schutz, *Reflections on the Problem of Relevance* (1945–1951), ed., annot., and introd. by Richard M. Zaner (New Haven and London: Yale University Press, 1970).

7. Brenda Venable Powell, "The What and Why of Experience: The Contrapuntal Relationship between Cognitive Style and Systems of Relevance," *The Annals of Phenomenological Sociology*, 2 (1977): 107–33; the quotation is from p. 120.

8. Alfred Schutz, "Husserl's Importance for the Social Sciences" (1959), CP I, pp. 140–9. Also see his earlier "Some Leading Concepts of Phenomenology" (1945), CP I, pp. 99–117, and the still earlier "Phenomenology and the Social Sciences" (1940), CP I, pp. 118–39.

9. I have long been puzzled by Schutz's use of "objective" here but have been able to think of only one surmise: that "objective" refers to the meaning which "something of the kind," "this sort of thing," a type, has at a given time and place, rather than the meaning that results from my effort to put myself in the shoes of its producer.

10. Alfred Schutz, *The Phenomenology of the Social World*, trans. by George Walsh and Frederick Lehnert, introd. by George Walsh (Evanston, IL: Northwestern University Press, 1967), chap. 4; originally *Der sinnhafte Aufbau der sozialen Welt* (1932), (Wien: Springer, 1960), Vierter Abschnitt.

11. Ibid., section 22, esp. p. 113; *"echtes Fremdverstehen": Der sinnhafte Aufbau*, esp. par. 22, p. 124.

12. Cf. ibid., Sec. 39; original, par. 39.

13. Georg Simmel, "How Is Society Possible?" (1908), trans. by Kurt H. Wolff, in *Georg Simmel, 1858–1918: A Collection of Essays with Translations and a Bibliography*, ed. by Wolff (Columbus, OH: Ohio State University Press, 1959), p. 342.

14. Alfred Schutz, "Common-Sense and Scientific Interpretation of Human Action" (1953), CP I, pp. 11–13, or "Symbol, Reality and Society" (1955), CP I, pp. 315–16.

15. The relevance of change introduces the problem of self-understanding, thus of continuity; but this can only be mentioned here.

16. Cf. Schutz, *The Phenomenology of the Social World*, p. 233; original, p. 266; "On Multiple Realities," pp. 249, 254, 255.

17. Schutz, "Phenomenology and the Social Sciences," p. 125, n. 6.

18. Edmund Husserl, *Cartesianische Meditationen und Pariser Vorträge* (1929 ff.; Den Haag: Nijhoff, 1950), p. 149; cf. Husserl, *Cartesian Meditations*, trans. by Dorion Cairns (The Hague: Nijhoff, 1960), p. 120. (Italics omitted.)

19. Alfred Schutz, "Sartre's Theory of the Alter Ego" (1948), CP I, pp. 195, 197.

20. Maurice Merleau-Ponty, *Phénoménologie de la perception* (Paris: Gallimard, 1945), p. i; cf. Merleau-Ponty, *Phenomenology of Perception*, trans. by Colin Smith (London: Routledge & Kegan Paul, 1962), p. vii. Also see Paul Ricoeur, "Husserl's Fifth Cartesian Meditation," in Ricoeur, *Husserl: An Analysis of His Phenomenology*, trans. by Edward G. Ballard and Lester E. Embree (Evanston, IL: Northwestern University Press, 1967), pp. 115–42.

21. Cf. this germane sweeping statement by Georg Simmel: "The history of philosophy shows the peculiar and not particularly praiseworthy fact that it has left unfulfilled its claim to provide a deeper assessment of life in regard to a number of the most important and problematic elements of life. Apart from occasional observations, it does not instruct us concerning the concept of fate, the enigmatic structure of what we call 'experiencing,' prior to Schopenhauer even the deep meaning for life of happiness and suffering in so far as this meaning is morally significant. Of the great vital powers, it has perhaps neglected love most—as if love were a kind of incidental matter, merely an adventure of the subjective soul, unworthy of the seriousness and rigorous objectivity of philosophical endeavor." Georg Simmel, "Der platonische und der moderne Eros" (? 1921), in Simmel, *Fragmente und Aufsätze aus dem Nachlass und Veröffentlichungen der letzten Jahre* (see fourth entry, n. 9), p. 127; cf. Donald N. Levine's almost identical translation in Simmel, *On Individuality and Social Forms*, ed. and introd. by Donald N. Levine (Chicago: University of Chicago Press, 1971), p. 235.

22. Schutz, "On Multiple Realities," p. 228, but also in many other places.

23. E.g., ibid., p. 220. In a subtle analysis of Schutz's treatment of the We-relation, Arthur S. Parsons has discovered a variant (comparable to Powell's discovery of a variant of world-definition-by-cognitive-style) which he calls the "transcendental We-relation" and which points to a more than cognitive intersubjectivity: Arthur S. Parsons, "Constitutive Phenomenology: Alfred Schutz's Theory of the We-Relation," *Journal of Phenomenological Psychology*, 4, 1 (Fall, 1973): 341–61, esp. the last section, "VI. The Two Modes of the We-Relation" (348–61).

24. Both in CP II.

25. Part of "Sinn einer Kunstform (Musik)," in Alfred Schutz, *Theorie der Lebensformen (Frühe Manuskripte aus der Bergson-Periode)*, ed. and introd. by Ilja Srubar (Frankfurt: Suhrkamp, 1981). The whole book, containing Schutz's writing during the years of Bergson's greatest influence on him and preceding *Der sinnhafte Aufbau*, awaits analysis in relation to Schutz's later work. Meanwhile Srubar's "Einleitung: Schütz' Bergson-Rezeption" is most helpful, as is Helmut R. Wagner's to his English translation: see n. 29 below.

26. In CP II.

27. Alfred Schutz and Thomas Luckmann, *The Structures of the Life-World*, trans. by Richard M. Zaner and H. Tristan Engelhardt, Jr. (Evanston, IL: Northwestern University Press, 1973).

28. Schutz, "On Multiple Realities," p. 255 (and elsewhere).

29. For a different but compatible critique of Schutz for his neglect of *praxis* (in the Marxian sense of Critical Theory), see Zygmunt Bauman, "In the Prevailing Circumstances" (on the occasion of Alfred Schutz, *Life Forms and Meaning Structure* [see the original cited in n. 25 above], trans., introd., and annot. by Helmut R. Wagner [London: Routledge & Kegan Paul, 1982]; and Burke C. Thomason, *Making Sense of Reification: Alfred Schutz and Constructionist Theory* [London: Macmillan, 1982]); *Times Literary Supplement*, 19 November 1982, p. 1283. The general thrust of Bauman's critique is similar to that of phenomenology more generally advanced by members of the Frankfurt School; see Kurt H. Wolff, "Phenomenology and Sociology," in *A History of Sociological Analysis*, ed. by Tom Bottomore and Robert Nisbet (New York: Basic Books, 1978), pp. 506–9. The analysis of the relation between Bauman's and the present critique remains to be worked out.

30. "Here [with this second question], you reached a core problem of the whole approach of Schutz to mutual understanding and intersubjectivity. It has occupied me for a long time. It is clear to me that Schutz, with his extraordinary capacity for friendship and all it entails—with, in every case since he left Vienna, rare and short personal encounters interspersed by sometimes close to [a] year or more intervals of spatial separation—considered this never a matter of self-observation and maintained a theoretical position which I explain by his adherence to some basic principles of Husserl: the exclusion of emotional experiences from phenomenological observation in favor of 'rational'—cognitive processes. (He knew better in his early Bergsonian days.) [Cf. Alfred Schutz, *Life Forms and Meaning Structure* (1924–1928).] And he was not quite comfortable with phenomenological rationalism either, as he showed when repeatedly praising Scheler for having concerned himself extensively with emotions." From a letter to the author by Helmut R. Wagner, 5 February 1983.

SIXTH ENTRY
KARL MANNHEIM

Karl Mannheim

I. Schutz, Mannheim, and the Task of This Entry

Schutz advocates the clearcut separation of analysis and feeling, of epistemology and Scheler's third kind of knowledge (philosophical, metaphysical, religious, redemptive), social-scientific investigation and personal relation—but we also saw that he could not maintain such a neat separation. He ignores and thus neglects the conflict between the two factors he explicitly wants to keep separate (belonging as they do to different "worlds"). Thus he embodies the conflict between advocacy of such separation and the fact of its impossibility. In a good society, there would be no such conflict; as I suggested in the third entry, the sociology (or social science) that would transcend it is inspired by commitment to a good society—and we add now, by commitment to the most scrupulous effort to articulate "commitment to a good society," that is to say, commitment to the most scrupulous effort to articulate "commitment" and "good society" as the ongoing precondition of both of them.

Both of these commitments, to a good society and to the articulations indicated, are quite explicit in Karl Mannheim. This was a factor in Schutz's negative attitude toward him, whose sociology of knowledge, with its focus on history and its Marxian elements, he contrasted with his own conception, which is best developed in his paper, "The Well-Informed Citizen: An Essay on the Social Distribution of Knowledge."[1] In this paper Schutz presents a typology of "men of knowledge," to use the term Florian Znaniecki employed for his own typology,[2] and neither study articulates the historical circumstances to which their types apply or in which they were conceived (there must be much overlap between these two historical circumstances). Related to Schutz's attitude toward

Mannheim's sociology of knowledge is his attitude toward the idea of surrender-and-catch, as Schutz's biographer Helmut R. Wagner has clearly seen.[3] Indeed, what the sociology of knowledge as understood by Mannheim (and by me) and surrender-and-catch have in common (among other things) are the aforementioned commitments.[4]

But now to Karl Mannheim himself. Because Mannheim has decisively influenced my own thinking, this—and it is quite in line with the conception of sociology here developing—is going to be the most personal entry into this sociology. I will argue, in fact, that it is important, and why it is important, to try to meet Mannheim, rather than talk about him as a third person—or, in Martin Buber's terms, to establish a "thou-" rather than an "it-relation" with him.[5] To this purpose, I shall have much to say about my own relation to him, during his life and since. For it is I who shall try to grasp the phenomenon he was, he is, and I shall try to do so in your presence, with you. What I hope, of course, and have faith in is that the encounter I shall try to establish goes beyond idiosyncracy and beyond the individuals, even the sociologists or philosophers or whoever else we may be, into the exemplary or typical, even universal. But we must begin with ourselves.

Ourselves? At once there is the question of who we are. It is a question that before we start thinking about it probably sounds silly or strange, without any bearing on our topic, "Karl Mannheim." But it is a crucial question. Here it means: are we gatherers of information about Karl Mannheim or do we want to establish a relation with Karl Mannheim? Most would opt for an affirmative answer to the first alternative: yes, we want information about Mannheim's work, about the significance of this work, particularly, perhaps, about its significance given our situation today, however defined. I shall urge, however, that at this moment in world history the best way to attain these aims is by choosing to affirm the second alternative, that is, to seek a relation with Mannheim.

The two approaches to our theme are qualitatively different. We cannot achieve a genuine relation to a thinker (or anybody or anything) by means of optimal information, and we cannot attain maximal knowledge by means of relating, no matter how closely. Still, the fact that the aims of the two approaches differ does not mean that one cannot be put at the service of the other. They seek different kinds of knowledge or truth—the first "existential" truth; the second, "scientific" truth,[6] and the best possible understanding would do right by both. But this cannot be the aim here. Here I want to show the importance of the neglected or abused approach to existential truth—neglected because considered unscientific, abused because it is thought to legitimate sentimentality and imprecision.

An encounter or a relation with Mannheim refers, as I hinted at, to "the phenomenon Karl Mennheim." "Phenomenon" is used here in the sense of the founder of phenomenology, Edmund Husserl: it is that which appears to us when we approach it in as unprejudiced a manner as we can muster or, in my own terms, when we surrender to it. Ideally, therefore, to try to establish a relation with Karl Mannheim means first to acquire enough knowledge about him, his work, his relations, influences on and by him and whatever else we may be able to imagine as potentially pertinent so that we would have a wealth of information to suspend. Then we should suspend (bracket) all of it as best we can to allow him to appear beyond the points of reference and frameworks we have acquainted ourselves with but have suspended because they have come from sources other than Karl Mannheim and therefore do not necessarily do justice to him: instead, they must be tested by being held in abeyance, suspended, bracketed. What we have *not* been able to bracket co-constitutes our object and our knowledge of it. The maximum suspension we can achieve is surrender to somebody, or something; and its result, outcome, harvest is the catch of the surrender.

In the attempt I want to make in this entry I endeavor to be the person who surrenders, and the hoped-for answer to the question of who we are is: the persons who surrender to this attempt at surrendering to the phenomenon Karl Mannheim.

A moment's reflection will show that surrender can only be a matter of degree. We cannot possibly suspend all our conceptions, views, certainties, hypotheses, or ideas because their sum total being our culture, it would mean to suspend our culture altogether, that is, to be reduced to a biological organism. In other words, we cannot ascertain how another human being truly is because in trying to do so we have nothing at our disposal except our culture, and this culture, by definition, is not that of any other human being. In this sense, surrender is necessarily a compromise, a compromise between the impossibility of approaching the other—if we were to shed all of our culture, which we cannot do anyway—and a distortion, inasmuch as no matter how far we can manage to go in suspending our notions, it cannot possibly be all the way.

II. Misgivings

Let me try another route to this point. I heard a very appealing lecture by a famous philosopher of science whose widely respected work I, too, admire. In his lecture, he was quite passionate about the historicity of scientific theorizing. In response, I suggested to him that this historicity is grounded in what may be called the paradox of socialization: we cannot do without socialization, in fact cannot imagine ourselves *being* without it, but at the same time socialization co-constitutes, and thus distorts, the world. Either nothing or a false picture. Or we can put this by saying that every perception is an interpretation; there is no such thing as "pure, uncontaminated" perception; no such thing as purely "*objektadäquate*" knowledge.

I myself [I added] have got to these problems by way of the sociology of knowledge (I studied with Karl Mannheim), crucially the question of the possibility of universal truth, or more sharply yet: the problem of relativism (not only epistemological but also—of course—moral).

I quote the bulk of the answer I received:

You say "socialization co-constitutes, and thus distorts the world. Either nothing or a false picture." I know why you say these things, and I find them tempting, too. But I also think they have to be wrong. If socialization co-constitutes the world, then that is what the world is like, and there can be no talk of distortion. If the alternative to a false picture is nothing, then the picture cannot properly be said to be false. The problem is an old one with me, and I still remember how disturbed I was when I encountered it in *Ideology and Utopia*, a book I have always greatly admired. But I also thought that Mannheim's attempts to recapture a positivistic notion of objectivity after having shown that nothing of the sort could exist created profound difficulties for his viewpoint. I cannot claim to be able to do vastly better myself, but I am still trying.

To repeat: after quoting my position, which I previously formulated here as the advocacy of surrender, though necessarily a compromise between the impossibility of approaching the other and the distortion of the other (and indeed of ourselves as well), and which in my letter I referred to as the paradox of socialization—"either nothing or a false picture"—my correspondent writes: "I know why you say these things, and I find them tempting, too. But I also think they have to be wrong." Why do they have to be wrong? My respondent's reply appears to imply a wish to turn away from surrender. For unlike the quest for scientific truth and, more obviously, for information in the ordinary sense of the term, surrender takes us out of the ordinary world, the *Lebenswelt*, Alfred Schutz's "paramount reality,"[7] or out of the scientific world, into the world that threatens us with having nothing to go by but ourselves as well as the other person who, however, is equally bared; a world in which we feel the threat of Nothing because All is at stake—the threat of death.[8]

To bring this even closer to home, alluding to the relevance of surrender to the grasp of our historical situation—which foreshadows my understanding of Mannheim's relevance for this situation—let me give one more example. Not long ago, at a conference on "The Emigration of German-speaking Social Scientists, 1933–1945, and Its Effect on German Postwar Sociology," I said in my contribution, " 'The Personal History of an Emigrant,' " that neither I nor anybody else can be exhaustively defined as an emigrant or an immigrant, indeed that, quite generally, the consciousness of a human being who fully identifies with his or her role is a false consciousness.

> In reality [I continued], such an identification is probably quite rare; I find it difficult, for instance, to imagine a craftsman or a factory worker or a physician who even as a husband, father, or citizen remains a craftsman, factory worker, or physician. But many social scientists, that is to say, explorers of human affairs, tend to identify with their role of explorers and thus to dehumanize whatever human problem they analyze. And if, as so often, this is human beings or a human being, the dehumanization which the researcher imposes on him- or herself is likely to be contagious: in view of the prestige of science and other characteristics of our society, these human beings take over the image that their investigator has of them and thus are dehumanized as well.

> To say this presupposes that a social-scientific view of the individual as, for instance, the sum of its roles, is replaced by a view that is based on the distinction between the social and the human, between the empirical subject and the transcendental subject.

While this last sentence points to one of the presuppositions of the idea of surrender, this is not the reason for presenting the quotation at this point. The reason is that it was perceived as a provocation: I had hardly finished my paper, and a prominent sociologist, of a phenomenological persuasion, visibly enraged, asked me whether I had ever met such a sociologist (who is always a sociologist) "in the flesh." I answered to the effect that most sociologists I knew did approximate the type. What is important here is the affinity of this reaction with my epistolary correspondent's insistence that while he knew why I said "those things" which he, too, found tempting, he thought nevertheless that "they have to be wrong." In the second example, loyalty to the "family" or organization of sociologists or the safety of positivistic thought structure or a combination of the two must have prevented the speaker from drawing the consequences of his own position as a phenomenologically formed thinker who might otherwise have held or come to hold a position quite similar to my own. Even though the statement I quoted was a very small part of my presentation and occurred in an early section, it must have lingered on, making for a reaction that masked the same anxiety I imputed to the first respondent I have mentioned.

III. Difficulties, Intrinsic and Contingent

I pointed out that in surrender we leave the everyday world and enter that which confronts us with the necessity of pulling ourselves up by our own bootstraps and of having to meet the other who has no other option either, a world in which we are vis-à-vis all-or-nothing.

This difficulty that inheres in surrender may suggest the problem of intersubjectivity, of transcendental intersubjectivity, for the fact is, to repeat, that our capacity to identify with the other, to know the other (but indeed, also to identify with myself, to know myself) cannot be complete but only one of degree; it cannot be absolute but only relative. This less than complete intersubjectivity characterizes not only everyday life but even surrender, whatever its occasion and whatever its theme. Both occasion and theme may be anything whatever, including matters incomparably harder to verbalize or formulate than the present occasion, Karl Mannheim.

This occasion, however, carries a second, quite contingent, difficulty. While the first difficulty is constitutive of surrender, of the human being, of human knowledge, the second is only embarrassing. It is that I am aware of being able to do no more than suggest what "surrender to Karl Mannheim" could be if I had more knowledge, even information, and more time. Thus the best I can hope to offer is *partem pro toto*, that is, even a smaller part than if I were more competent and had more time.

IV. Mannheim as a Teacher

I said that in my effort, in our effort, to establish an encounter with Karl Mannheim, I must start out with my own relation to him, during his life and afterward, since it is I who shall try to grasp the phenomenon he was and is and "shall try to do so in your presence, with you." In the meantime, I have said (again) something about surrender; now we can embark on our journey proper.

In 1930, after graduating from the *Realgymnasium* in Darmstadt, I entered the university in nearby Frankfurt without knowing what I wanted to study. I took quite an assortment of courses, but after a semester or two, somebody, probably a fellow student, told me (I don't remember him or her, and perhaps it was no more than a rumor)—in short: I absolutely must hear that new professor who had just arrived from Heidelberg. I went, mostly out of curiosity, but was at once fascinated, above all, by two things (either God's ways are mysterious, or it was the cunning of reason): Mannheim's Hungarian accent and what seemed to me silk shirts. Later in seminars, after I had been impressed even more, I was struck by another peculiarity: he consumed unlit cigarettes by sucking and chewing them. It didn't in the least occur to me to inquire into the reasons for his appearance and his habits, I just took it all in. There was something in Mannheim that fascinated me and that made me hang on to his accent, his shirts, his cigarette mush. Today, it seems to me that it prepared me for surrender, the experience itself as well as the conceptualization of the experience. The catch of this surrender to Karl Mannheim thus is what has become my vocation, and not only as this vocation manifests itself in sociology. Sociology was the arena where I developed the idea of surrender-and-catch and went beyond: gradually, Mannheim for me came to stand above all for the undismayed and undismayable exploration of whatever might be a candidate for exploration, without, however, in any way denying the existence of the mysterious. When I studied with him (1930–1933), I remember that I also thought he secretly was a poet and I was thrilled by the idea, but as far as I know the only writing of his that approaches poetry is *Die Dame aus Biarritz*, an unpublished play (1920) that suggests influences of Wedekind, Ibsen, and Strindberg. In the romantic-adolescent longing it portrays it once or twice waxes poetic—it even rhymes! But I have come to think, much later indeed, that the passage at the end of his famous essay—with which the whole discussion of Mannheim, the "sociology of knowledge dispute," [9] began, the paper he presented at the sixth German sociology congress in Zurich in 1928—"Competition as a Cultural Phenomenon" [10] comes close to what for me is the phenomenon Karl Mannheim. To adopt the sociological viewpoint, he wrote,

> does not mean to say that mind and thought are nothing but the expression and reflex of various "locations" in the social fabric, and that there exist only quantitatively determinable functional correlations and no potentiality of "freedom" grounded in mind; it merely means that even within the sphere of the intellectual, there are processes amenable to rational analysis, and that it would be an ill-advised mysticism which would shroud things in romantic obscurity at a point where rational cognition is still practicable. Anyone who wants to drag in the irrational where the lucidity and acuity of reason still must rule by right merely shows that he is afraid to face the mystery at its legitimate place. [11]

By this time, in 1928, when Mannheim was still in Heidelberg, he had become a sociologist. A reading of his preceding papers allows us to trace the itinerary from the "Sunday Circle" in Budapest[12] and his first essays that he wrote in Hungarian, such as "Soul and Culture" (1918),[13] through his early thoughts on "The Distinctive Character of Cultural-Sociological Knowledge," on "A Sociological Theory of Culture and Its

Knowability (Conjunctive and Communicative Thinking)," [14] and on interpretation,[15] to his better-known papers—"Historicism" (1924), "The Problem of a Sociology of Knowledge" (1925), and the first of his three books, the most famous one, *Ideology and Utopia* (1929). The other two, *Man and Society in an Age of Reconstruction* (1935, 1940) and the posthumously published *Freedom, Power and Democratic Planning* (1950), belong to a later phase, usually referred to as the planning phase. But Mannheim himself echoes through all of his work, from Hungary through Germany to England.

V. Mysticism the Conscience of Philosophy

To make this more obvious I shall quote at length from a very early piece (1919), Mannheim's review of Ernst Bloch's *Geist der Utopie*. Its affinity with the quotation from "Competition as a Cultural Phenomenon" of nine years later may be clear even on a first reading, but I shall comment on it after presenting the text.

It is important that in this book is again made visible and brought to consciousness in modern formulation the fact that there is one unconstruable question the essence of which is that it can never be attained in a concrete form because it transcends every approach to a problem that can be pursued by the intellect but that it is a given nevertheless because it is traceable in every great metaphysic as guiding the movement of its problem, as the unshakable longing of which already Plato speaks. The existence of this unconstruable question is recognized by the negative theology of the Middle Ages when it points to there being things of which we have no adequate concepts; and so does the idea of the "coincidentia oppositorum" indicate it by locating the attainability of the unattainable beyond thesis-antithesis thinking. The confessions of the mystics and ecstatics seek to let this utterly unattainable appear through the method of exclusion; only the path that leads there and what comes afterward are described in these confessions, and in the place left empty between the two there is at least suggested the *topos* of the inexpressible.

But not only mysticism is occupied with this unattainable, for it has been the point of departure of every great philosophy, whether its question be what the essence of the world is or who I am. It is the tragedy of the history of philosophy and often of particular thinkers, too, that with their construable questions they rather move away from the unconstruable one because when one enters the path of concrete formulation one is forced to follow the consequences which result from this formulation. When we are still where we raise the question of the essence of the world and of ourselves and in its utter simplicity this question is pure and naive, there still lives in it the astonishment of the admiration by which we become conscious of ourselves. But when this question turns into its own purpose and instead of asking naively we ask about the essence of the world as that element which meets all requirements that follow from the *concept* of essence, or when we ask what the character of this essence must be for it to be knowable, then we have pushed the astonishment that spontaneously wells up onto the ready-made conceptual track of the solvability of problems; the question rolls on all by itself, and we follow it to where we really have no business. In the course of the history of ideas we can observe how into the place of unanswerable questions others insinuate themselves to which our answer is possible or already available. Questions of logic and epistemology replace pure wonderment and let us forget the earlier ultimate sense of the question, presenting us with their own attainable answers. In this fashion, the knowledge of the world and things replaces our restlessness in which we seek God and ourselves.

By contrast, mysticism has always been the conscience of philosophy because it keeps on reminding us of the ultimate questions. For this reason the philosophical specialist is so nervous about it; he feels that it reminds him of an old promise which he does not want to fulfill. Bloch's book also has this significance: that it revives this promise in contemporary philosophy. He, too, stands in this mystical-esoteric historical continuity which has always accompanied, as a live conscience within the development of philosophy, its analytic and systematizing tendency.[16]

If the 1928 passage is put together with this (neither of which was known to me fifty years ago, at the time when after a short while of knowing Karl Mannheim I somehow suspected him of secretly being a poet), then such a hunch becomes more plausible. I cannot recall anything in particular he had said which would influence my hunch, but his sympathetic understanding of mystics and ecstatics, his elevation of mysticism to the status of conscience of philosophy, his insistence on the "unconstruable question," his observation that the history of philosophy was characterized by replacing—prematurely? from weakness? impatiently? because of a need for closure?—the unconstruable question by construable ones whose answers are ready—all of this (and more) points to a full appreciation of the mysterious but at the same time to a shyness to admit it and to an all the more passionate desire to go as far as possible in his analysis, rather than dragging "in the irrational where the lucidity and acuity of reason still must rule by right." That I called this syndrome that of a poet had to do with my conception of poetry during that *Sturm und Drang* period of mine; but the intimate relationship between poetry and philosophy—precisely not, to be sure, the job of "the philosophical specialist"—has stayed with me and is, I now realize, a central element in the idea of surrender-and-catch.[17]

VI. Rilke's First Sonnet to Orpheus

Mannheim must have had a hunch of my notion of him because one day he approached me with the suggestion that I think about the problem of "*Sich haben*," literally the problem of "having oneself." I did not understand what he meant and I remember that he tried several formulations which I don't recall but which referred (unless I make this up now) to the way a person sees him- or herself or perhaps changes the very conception of identity. Without being clear (or now remembering why), I began the task Mannheim had suggested by reading the first of Rainer Maria Rilke's *Sonette an Orpheus*, scribbling all over the page so that the page (the only one I so disfigured in Nr. 115 of the "Insel Bücherei") looked like the small space of a sacred text surrounded by commentary. I reproduce, in translation, my scribbles but must first quote the sonnet:

> Da stieg ein Baum. O reine Übersteigung!
> O Orpheus singt! O hoher Baum im Ohr!
> Und alles schwieg. Doch selbst in der Verschweigung
> ging neuer Anfang, Wink und Wandlung vor.
>
> Tiere aus Stille drangen aus dem klaren
> gelösten Wald von Lager und Genist;
> und da ergab sich, dass sie nicht aus List
> und nicht aus Angst in sich so leise waren,
>
> sondern aus Hören. Brüllen, Schrei, Geröhr
> schien klein in ihren Herzen. Und wo eben
> kaum eine Hütte war, dies zu empfangen,
>
> ein Unterschlupf aus dunkelstem Verlangen
> mit einem Zugang, dessen Pfosten beben,
> da schufst du ihnen Tempel im Gehör.[18]

I commented (ever so tentatively, searchingly):

Designation of the kind of interpretation. [I must have been under the sway of Mannheim's distinction between "immanent" and "transcendent" interpretation; cf. his paper mentioned in n. 15 above.] Though immanent as interpretation, within the immanence, however, there rises the question of why the poet has spoken in just this or that way. [This could mean: from immanent to transcendent interpretation—or as I later was to change my terminology, from intrinsic to extrinsic interpretation.] But not so simple here: the poet [is] inseparable so that he, too, [is] immanent.

[On the margin of the first stanza:] We have the feeling [of] the word itself. Transition from the naive consideration that is dictated by the everyday [world] to that which is adequate to poetry: to that space in which the word can no longer be accomplished ["vollziehbar"] but in which it mediates directly in [the poet's] drunkenness [Rausch]. To examine: (1) why just the word, (2) why just these words?

[On the margin of the second stanza:] Why precisely animal in the beginning?

Characteristic of Rilke! But the locus of this question must first be ascertained.

[I made an arrow from *Angst* to *Hören*.] Road from everyday to the idea [Einfall]!! (Sketchy!!)

[Following the third stanza, with *Hütte* underscored:] Change of objects through the idea [Einfall], demonstrated by the *inspired* [*eingefallenen*] receptacle of the idea [Einfall-Empfangsgerät].

[Alongside the last two stanzas:] Experienced tendency (after the experience of poetry as deproblematization) to deproblematization: the "pure word" (Platonic Idea)—*Word* must still be interpreted.

[At the end of the last line of the sonnet:] What is meant by Gehör [hearing]?

[Following the sonnet (on the same page):] Poetry in principle deproblematization. This expression only has become schematic today, that is, the way to it is not indicated. But it [the way] has of course been made by way of the way, [coming] exactly from poetry which, that is, has discovered and designated it in its naive accomplishing only very late, perhaps altogether not yet.

[Arrow from *Angst*:] To assure himself of this fundamental deproblematizing again and again is Rilke's impulse. He never *has himself* in anxiety, he *has himself* only in the idea [*Einfall*; to this word leads a line from *Hören*. *Brüllen, Schrei, Geröhr,* and *Hören* has a line to *Angst*] which, precisely, no longer admits of any problem. To this is added the form of the anxiety which is too nameless to remain such and for this reason is objectified by metaphors (animal) and by instinctive analogies (howling, cry, roar).

But poetry as deproblematization is an interpretation adequate to its sense only. To be considered also, however, is the socially relevant meaning of poetry; this [is] the direction of interpretation![19]

VII. Intrinsic and Extrinsic Interpretation

It may seem that this report on my effort to make sense of Mannheim's suggestion to explore how different kinds of people "have themselves" by giving into my fascination with Rilke's *Sonnets to Orpheus* has nothing to do with my theme, which is the phenomenon Karl Mannheim. On the contrary, it is essential—or, more precisely, it is, to my own surprise, the catch, at least part of the catch, of my surrendering to this theme. In the first place, my scribbles on the margins of Rilke's poem bear witness to my surrender to this poem and thus show what I mean by surrender to something: I could say it means getting into it, and coming out of it changed. However disappointing the scribbles may be, they show (as do further thoughts detailed in note 19), in the second place, how absorbed I was by some of Mannheim's ideas about interpretation, especially the distinction between *intrinsic* and *extrinsic*. To interpret intrinsically ("immanently") means to mine the interpretandum, in this case a text in the literal sense of the term, without to the best of one's ability using ideas not originating in it. But since we have to use words that are not coined on the occasion but come from outside the interpretandum, and since we have to use particular words, namely, words that function within conceptions, hypotheses, theories that we must enlist for the sake of making sense of the text, we cannot do without such extrinsic help. Extrinsic, in contrast to intrinsic, interpretation means one that resorts to something outside the interpretandum—such as a theory, a frame of reference, an interest that directs selective attention to it—e.g., the writer's biography or significant experiences, position in a certain tradition, even race or climate. But, obviously, such an interpretation cannot be undertaken except of an interpretandum that must, necessarily, have been interpreted in a preliminary fashion intrinsically because otherwise the interpreter would not know what to ask and thus whether to go outside or where outside. The distinction between the two kinds of interpretation can thus be no more than relative since in each of them we need the other. Nevertheless, the distinction is of great importance. It is one of intent, and the intent of the maximally feasible intrinsic interpretation is the surrender to the interpretandum, such as I, long before I used the term, practiced in my, surely rather unsuccessful, effort to read Rilke's poem. This I did, to repeat, as a consequence of Mannheim's assignment and under the influence of his thoughts on interpretation. (Many years later, I translated his paper on the subject [see note 15].)

VIII. Diagnosis of Our Time

In a literal sense not as long-lasting as my view on interpretation was my concern with the idea and above all the fact of *labilization*. I have no proof, but I must have picked up the word from Mannheim, probably from a lecture since I have not come across it in his publications. As the term suggests, it refers to the disappearance or weakening of any stable order of norms, principles, guidelines, or traditions which instead have become "labile."

> Things fall apart; the centre cannot hold;
> Mere anarchy is loosed upon the world,
> The blood-dimmed tide is loosed, and everywhere
> The ceremony of innocence is drowned;
> The best lack all conviction, while the worst
> Are full of passionate intensity.[20]

Labilization is a notion closely related to Mannheim's relativism; for me, it has turned out as a challenge—a challenge which, I realize by hindsight, I have tried to meet using the idea of surrender-and-catch. "I, I felt, had no scheme at all; I wanted to *know*," I wrote in "Surrender and Catch" (1950), the short piece that gave rise to all that has since followed on the topic.[21] A very strong component of the desire to know is where we, humanity, are at this historical moment. This component has become incomparably stronger with the growth of the nuclear industry: for the first time in our history we are able to destroy ourselves and our planet—something that until a few years ago only nonhuman-inhuman nature was capable of.

Labilization and what I just added are diagnostic of our time, and "the diagnosis of our time" was one of Mannheim's leitmotifs throughout his career. Was a Marxist diagnosis adequate? He considered it and gave it its place but no monopoly,[22] and so he should have done if he indeed stood for what I had come to think he did: for "undismayed and undismayable exploration" (see IV above). His whole sociology of knowledge was diagnostic, even in its technical epistemological concerns, the center of which was the question of how we think and how, given our circumstances, we should think, as we shall see more clearly in the next section. Or take the ideology-utopia syndrome and see its diagnostic nature. Both ideology and utopia are "existence-transcending," Mannheim thought, but according to the last lines of *Ideologie and Utopie*,[23] the decline of ideology would be critical only for some groups, while (as I wrote elsewhere) the decline of utopia

would change men into things. Ideology presupposes a point of view, whose unveiling or unmasking, which shows its partiality, clarifies matters, broadens the mind, and in the sense of the Enlightenment, can make us more mature. . . . But . . . [there is an] implied identification of unveiling and abolishing: as long as there is no complete "congruence with existence," there are points of view, perspectives, hence ideologies. . . . In fact, utopia, which compared with ideology so broadly conceived as Mannheim does here, is a much more particular kind of transcendence, can disappear without requiring the disappearance of standpoints. Hence Mannheim's alternative—the decline of one or the other—is illogical on his own terms. The correct alternatives at first glance appear to be two: first, complete congruence with existence, hence neither ideology nor utopia, as against a transcendable world, which thus has ideologies and the possibility of utopia—but since the first term is unimaginable [surrender can be only a matter of degree: see I above], this alternative turns out to be a mirage and collapses. There thus remains only the alternative ideology *and* utopia vs. ideology and *no* utopia, and this is not only realistic but timely today, when many believe that we have much ideology and many ideologies but no utopias. (The notion "the end of ideology," of course, is misleading and irrelevant here, since it refers to the end of a particular ideology or particular ideologies.) The explanation of Mannheim's fictitious alternative is that "utopia" figures in it as spirit, and "ideology" as belonging in society, as society: if he has to choose between spirit and society, he sides with the spirit. Yet even in this formulation, the alternative, of course, is a false one—Mannheim's "ecstasy" may here have got the better of him.[24]

This polarity between "spirit" and "society" moved in the course of his life from the former to the latter. In his Hungarian phase, the spirit dominated his interests and activities, as it did in his German writing, which shows, however, some examples of concern with social circumstances.[25] In England, however, his main concern was how to save society, how to create an affirmable society, as his writings, and especially his two books written in England, show. The reason for the comparatively slight shift in Germany probably was his increasing recognition, and in England, it was the advent and threatening victory of Nazism. As early as 1930 (in "On the Nature of Economic Ambition and Its Significance for the Social Education of Man"[26]), we "have an indication that Mannheim will devote himself ever more singlemindedly to thinking about the salvation of society, lest the spirit itself perish."[27] In what must have been a terrible shock—Nazism and what it ever less deniably forebode—he even marshalled religion in the service of the "planned society" without (to my mind) becoming a "neoconservative" or "more conservative with age." He was a kind of sociological consultant to "The Moot," a group among whose most widely known members were J. Middleton Murry and T. S. Eliot. Eliot wrote that "No contemporary thinker has more enriched my mental life in this way [making "German thought available to disagree with"] than Dr. Mannheim, to whom I feel I owe a considerable debt."[28]

IX. Relativism

It has been widely remarked that in his German phase Mannheim was unable to resolve the problem of relativism. In his first paper on the sociology of knowledge (1925), he was in so pioneering a spirit that he failed to see the problem of a universal truth—perhaps he took universal truth for granted. "In any case," he wrote,

We would like to go on record, at this point, that we cannot share the at present widespread fear of relativism. "Relativism" has become a catchword which, it is believed, will instantly annihilate any adversary against whom it is used. But as to us, we definitely prefer a "relativism" which accentuates the difficulty of its task by calling attention to all those moments which tend to make the propositions actually discoverable at any given time, partial and situationally conditioned—we prefer such a "relativism to an "absolutism" which loudly proclaims, as a matter of principle, the absoluteness of its own position or of "truth in itself," but is in fact no less partial than any of its adversaries—and, still worse, is utterly incapable of tackling with its epistemological apparatus the problem of the temporal and situational determination of any concrete process of thought, completely overlooking the way in which this situational conditioning enters into the structure and the evolution of knowledge.[29]

But in 1946, a few months before his death, he wrote:

If there are contradictions and inconsistencies in my paper this is, I think, not so much due to the fact that I overlooked them but because I make a point of developing a theme to its end even if it contradicts some other statements. I use this method because I think that in this marginal field of human knowledge we should not conceal inconsistencies, so to speak covering up the wounds, but our duty is to show the sore spots in human thinking at its present stage.

. . . In our empirical investigations we become aware of the fact that we are observing the world from a moving staircase, from a dynamic platform, and, therefore, the image of the world changes with the changing frames of reference which various cultures create . . . that you can only see various perspectives of a house and there is no view among them which is absolutely the house and in spite of that there is knowing because the various perspectives are not arbitrary. The one can be understood from the other. What we, without any difficulty, admit for the apperception of the visual world, we ought to admit for knowledge in general.

I hope this is intelligible and it at least convinced you and your seminar that if there are contradictions they are not due to my shortsightedness but to the fact that I want to break through the old epistemology radically but have not succeeded yet fully. But the latter is not one man's work. I think our whole generation will have to work on it as nothing is more obvious than that we transcend in every field the idea that man's mind is equal to an absolute Ratio in favour of a theory that we think on the basis of changing frames of reference, the elaboration of which is one of the most exciting tasks of the near future.[30]

While now there is admission of "contradictions and inconsistencies," their resolution "is not one man's work." But the nature of the contradictions is not spelled out. I don't see so much contradictions as the failure to recognize the question of what the "changing frames of reference" *have in common* which could account for their mutual translatability so that *all of us* can speak of "the house." It seems to me that Mannheim forgets, as it were, two essential elements of any epistemology: an objective external world, on the one hand, and reason as a universal human faculty on the other. The absence of these two components invalidates his own epistemology—and should be a lesson to us.

And the same absence reemerges in his English phase in the failure to answer the question, who plans the planners of his planned society, and how can they be prevented from abusing their power?[31] That is to say there is no consensus, either in Mannheim's or in our own society, that is strong enough so we take it for granted that our endowment with reason is a constant that sets the limit to both epistemological and moral relativism, that we must respect this universal human faculty which is our only means, directly or in its derivations and translations, of coming to terms with ourselves in our historical situation and with our environment, rather than destroying both. Mannheim's lifelong devotion to exploring and saving both spirit and society, moving if not tragic as it is, was handicapped by his failure to recognize and analyze the distrust of reason and the alienation from objective reality that is associated with it: it evinces them.

X. Translatability of the Catch

This, then, is my preliminary and rather breathless catch of my surrender to the phenomenon Karl Mannheim. It is mine, nobody else's; no two catches to the presumably "same" phenomenon are alike, nor can they be alike, because no two socializations are alike. But since surrendering to something claims the whole person, the human being in the person, and since this is the element common to all catches, they are translatable one into the other.[32] Such translation is undertaken in dialogue, two individuals speaking to one another, in the "clean" sense of the badly misused terms "dialogue" and "speaking with one another."[33] I hope that this discussion of Mannheim's significance for our situation may have found here a possible point from which to begin such talk.

Notes

1. Alfred Schutz, "The Well-Informed Citizen: An Essay on the Social Distribution of Knowledge" (1946), in *Collected Papers*, vol. 2, ed. and introd. by Arvid Brodersen (The Hague: Nijhoff, 1964), pp. 120–34. Also see Jonathan B. Imber, "The Well-Informed Citizen: Alfred Schutz and Applied Theory," *Human Studies* 7 (1984): 117–26.
2. Florian Znaniecki, *The Social Role of the Man of Knowledge* (New York: Columbia University Press, 1940). (A sociological comparison of these two typologies may yield worthwhile insights.)
3. Helmut R. Wagner, *Alfred Schutz: An Intellectual Biography* (Chicago:

University of Chicago Press, 1983), pp. 243–9. On my gradual discovery of both Schutz's and Mannheim's influence on my own thought, see "On My Brush with Phenomenology," in *American Phenomenology: Origins and Development* (*Analecta Husserliana*, vol. XXVI), ed. by E. F. Kaelin and C. O. Schrag (Dordrecht, Boston, London: Kluwer, 1989), pp. 442–5, esp. 443–4. Also see Wagner, "Between Ideal Type and Surrender: Field Research as Asymmetrical Relation," *Human Studies*, 1 (1978): 153–64.

4. See "The Sociology of Knowledge and Surrender-and-Catch" (1982), in *Beyond the Sociology of Knowledge: An Introduction and a Development* (Lanham, New York, London: University Press of America, 1983), pp. 256–67.

5. Martin Buber, *I and Thou* (1936), trans. by Ronald Gregor Smith (New York: Scribner's, 1958).

6. See *Beyond the Sociology of Knowledge*, esp. pp. 40–3, and *Surrender and Catch: Experience and Inquiry Today* (Dordrecht and Boston: D. Reidel, 1976), esp. pp. 128, 132–5.

7. See the first entry.

8. This is convincingly formulated in a Lacanian perspective in Judith Feher, "On Surrender, Death, and the Sociology of Knowledge," *Human Studies* 7, 2 (1984): 211–26.

9. Volker Meja and Nico Stehr, eds., *Der Streit um die Wissenssoziologie*, 2 vols. (Frankfurt: Suhrkamp, 1982). A selected English translation is to be published by Routledge & Kegan Paul.

10. In Mannheim, *Essays on the Sociology of Knowledge*, ed. [and trans.] by Paul Kecskemeti (London: Routledge and Kegan Paul; New York: Oxford University Press, 1952), pp. 191–229.

11. Ibid., p. 299; also in *From Karl Mannheim*, ed. and introd. by Kurt H. Wolff (New York: Oxford University Press, 1971), pp. 260–1. See also ibid., "Introduction: A Reading of Karl Mannheim," pp. xiii (the passage "might serve as a motto to much of Mannheim's work"), xlv, lvi; "Karl Mannheim," in *Klassiker des soziologischen Denkens, Zweiter Band, Von Weber bis Mannheim*, ed. by Dirk Käsler (München: Beck, 1978), pp. 288–9.

12. Cf. David Kettler, *Marxismus und Kultur: Mannheim und Lukács in den ungarischen Revolutionen 1918/19* (Neuwied und Berlin: Luchterhand, 1967); "Culture and Revolution," *Telos* 10 (Winter 1971): 35–92 (a revision, in English, of the preceding short book); Joseph Gabel, "Mannheim et le marxisme hongrois" (1969), in Gabel, *Idéologies* (Paris: Editions Anthropos, 1974), pp. 255–78; "Marxisme hongrois, hungaro-marxisme et École de Budapest," in Gabel, *Idéologies II* (Paris: Editions Anthropos, 1978), pp. 97–126, esp. 109–10; Éva Karádi and Erzsébet Vezér, eds., *Georg Lukács, Karl Mannheim und der Sonntagskreis*, trans. from the Hungarian by Albrecht Friedrich (Frankfurt a.M.: Sendler, 1985); Mary Gluck, *Georg Lukács and His Generation 1900–1918* (Cambridge, Mass., and London: Harvard University Press, 1985) (also contains instructive illustrations); and illustrations dominate the "picture book" *György Lukács: His Life in Pictures and Documents*, compiled and ed. by Éva Fekete and Éva Karádi (Budapest: Corvina Kiadó, 1981). Reproductions of photographs of Mannheim at the time of the "Sunday Circle" (two of them in *His Life in Pictures*, p. 70, one of them reproduced on the cover of Karádi and Vezér) and

later—surprisingly few are published—as in Mannheim, *Wissenssoziologie*, ed. introd. by Kurt H. Wolff (Berlin and Neuwied: Luchterhand, 1964) (cover) or in *From Karl Mannheim* (frontispiece), would help to render "more visible" the points I am trying to make here.

13. German translation by Ernest Manheim in Karl Mannheim, *Wissenssoziologie*, pp. 66–84. For an unpublished English version by "Mrs. Goodman" and the editor, L. Charles Cooper, see Appendix F, unpaged, in Cooper, *The Hindu Prince: A Sociological Biography of Karl Mannheim, 1893–1947*, unpublished and undated.

14. The two papers were posthumously published, edited and introduced by David Kettler, Volker Meja, and Nico Stehr, first in their original German as Mannheim, *Die Strukturen des Denkens* (Frankfurt: Suhrkamp, 1980), then in English as *Structures of Thinking*, trans. by Jeremy J. Shapiro and Shierry Weber Nicholsen (London: Routledge & Kegan Paul, 1982).

15. "The Ideological and the Sociological Interpretation of Intellectual Phenomena" (1926), trans. by Kurt H. Wolff, in *From Karl Mannheim*, pp. 116–31.

16. Karl Mannheim, "Ernst Bloch: Geist der Utopie," trans. into German from the Hungarian by Éva Karádi and Erzsébet Vezér, in Karádi and Vezér, *Georg Lukács, Karl Mannheim und der Sonntagshreis* (n. 12), pp. 254–5. An English version is contained in Cooper, *The Hindu Prince* (n. 13), translator not identified, Appendix I, unpaged, but the German translation appears to me more faithful to the original—which, unfortunately, I cannot read. Thus I made my own translation from the German one. But despite all the problems such an undertaking involves, they cannot be cause of a scandal like that of the French translation of *Ideologie und Utopie* from the English translation, which is a book quite different from the original. Cf. Gabel, "Mannheim et le marxisme hongrois," pp. 259–63, and on the differences between the German original and *Ideology and Utopia*, Wolff, "Introduction: A Reading of Karl Mannheim," in *From Karl Mannheim*, pp. lxi–lxv. I hope that in my own translation from the German translation of Mannheim's Hungarian review, his thrust as of that time comes out beyond all difficulties and, probably, errors involved in this hazardous venture.

17. I have tried to trace this and cognate relations in "Exploring Relations between Surrender-and-Catch and Poetry, Sociology, Evil," *Human Studies* 9 (1986): 347–64.

18. Here are three translations (I will not stop now to seek others):

A tree rising. What a pure growing!
Orpheus is singing! A tree inside the ear!
Silence, silence. Yet new buildings,
signals, and changes went on in the silence.

Animals created by silence came forward from the clear
and relaxed forest where their lairs were,
and it turned out the reason they were so full of silence
was not cunning, and not terror.

It was listening. Growling, yelping, grunting now
seemed all nonsense to them. And where before
there was hardly a shed where this listening could go,

a rough shelter put up out of brushy longings,
with an entrance gate whose poles were wobbly,
you created a temple for them deep inside their ears.
    (*Selected Poems of Rainer Maria Rilke*, a translation from the German
    and commentary by Robert Bly (New York: Harper & Row, 1981),
    p. 195.)

There arose a tree. Oh, pure transcension!
Oh, Orpheus sings! Oh, tall tree in the ear!
And all was still. But even in this suspension
new beginnings, signs, and changes were.

Animals from the silence, from the clear
now opened wood came forth from nest and den;
and it so came to pass that not from fear
or craftiness were they so quiet then,

but to be listening. Howling, cry, roar
seemed little to their hearts. Where scarce a humble
hut for such reception was before

a hiding-place of the obscurest yearning,
with entrance shaft whose underpinnings tremble.
you made for the beasts temples in the hearing.
    (Rainer Maria Rilke, *Sonnets to Orpheus*, with English translations
    by C. F. MacIntyre (Berkeley: University of California Press, 1960),
    p. 3.)

A tree stood up. Oh pure uprising!
Orpheus is singing! Oh tall tree in the ear!
And everything grew still. Yet in the silence there
changes took place, signals and fresh beginnings.

Creatures of stillness crowded from the clear
untangled woods, from nests and lairs;
and it turned out that their light stepping
came not from fear or from cunning

but so they could listen. Shriek, bellow and roar
had shrunk in their hearts. And while before
there was scarcely a hut where they might stay,

just a shelter made of the darkest cravings
with shaky posts for an entranceway—
you made a temple for them in their hearing.
    (Translated by David Young, *Field* 19 [Fall, 1978]: 77. I owe this
    reference to Alan Mandell, to whom I am grateful.)

19. I was surprised to find, a few weeks after I had written the first version of
    this essay, that I had done more about the problem of having oneself than
    framing Rilke's poem in tiny scribbles: I had typed a three-page outline
    which I grandiloquently titled (in German, of course): "Theoretical Foun-
    dation of the Problem of Having-Onself." (I no longer know whether I
    wrote this before or after the "commentary" on Rilke.) The "theoretical
    foundation" consists of three parts: "1. How is it that we raise the question

of having-onself? 2.a. Examples of contents of having-oneself, or forms, of having-oneself. b. Definition of the concept of having-oneself. 3. Relation of having-oneself to sociology." The definition: "Having-oneself . . . is the decisive . . . point from which to look at the total phenomenon of a given human being in order to understand as much as possible, whereby a life may have an indefinite number of forms of having-oneself (presumably in temporal sequence)." And the relation of having-oneself to sociology: "3. The central thesis is: Having oneself is not an immanently psychological affair but depends on our life space, which in turn depends on its sociological structure." And I conclude this sketch by declaring that "we" have chosen a historical period, that of the German *Sturm und Drang*, to analyze in regard to forms of having oneself.

I still have the books by authors of that period that I then bought and read, and I may even have some notes. But aside from whatever pertinence my precocious "outline" may have, I now discover in the idea of having-oneself a definition of the forerunner of the notion of "central attitude" that I developed in the early 40s. Both are meant to be concepts for the facilitation of understanding and thus, in their particular formulation, point to or anticipate "surrender." For the idea of central attitude (and related ideas), see my first paper on the sociology of knowledge, written ten to thirteen years after that then almost certainly forgotten "theoretical foundation, " "The Sociology of Knowledge: Emphasis on an Empirical Attitude" (1943), in *Beyond the Sociology of Knowledge*, pp. 106–31. And see "Die Form des Sich-Habens bei Rilke" (1932), in *Das Unumgängliche* (second entry, n. 1), pp. 136–44.

20. From Yeats's "The Second Coming."
21. "Surrender and Catch," in *Surrender and Catch*, pp. 9–17, at p. 9.
22. See, for example, his remarks at the seminar on Lukács's *Geschichte und Klassenbewusstsein*, held by Alfred Weber and Karl Mannheim in Heidelberg, 1929, excerpts of which are found in Karádi and Vezér, *Georg Lukács, Karl Mannheim und der Sonntagskreis* (see n. 12), pp. 298–303. The question of Mannheim's "Marxism" exercised the "sociology of knowledge dispute" (cf. n. 9).
23. Original edition, *Ideologie und Utopie* (Bonn: Friedrich Cohen, 1929), pp. 249–50. English edition, *Ideology and Utopia*, trans. by Louis Wirth and Edward Shils (New York: Harcourt, Brace, 1936), p. 236.
24. Wolff, "Introduction: A Reading of Karl Mannheim," pp. lxviii–lxix.
25. E.g., "Zur Problematik der Soziologie in Deutschland" (1929), in Mannheim, *Wissenssoziologie*, pp. 614–24; *Die Gegenwartsaufgaben der Soziologie: ihre Lehrgestalt* (Tübingen: Mohr, 1932); review of Stuart A. Rice, ed., *Methods in Social Science, American Journal of Sociology* 37 (1932): 273–82; "German Sociology (1918–1933)," *Politica* 1 (1934): 12–33.
26. In *Essays on the Sociology of Knowledge*, pp. 230–75.
27. Wolff, "Introduction: A Reading of Karl Mannheim," pp. lx–lxi.
28. Quoted in A. P. Simonds, *Karl Mannheim's Sociology of Knowledge* (Oxford: Clarendon Press, 1978), p. 1. See Eliot, *Notes towards the Definition of Culture* (New York: Harcourt, Brace, 1949), Preface. On The Moot more generally, see Bramsted and Gerth, "A Note on the Work of Karl Mannheim," in Mannheim, *Freedom, Power, and Democratic Planning*, ed. Ernest K. Bramsted and Hans Gerth (New York: Oxford University Press, 1950), pp. xiv–xv.

29. Karl Mannheim, "The Problem of a Sociology of Knowledge," in *Essays on the Sociology of Knowledge*, p. 137n.

30. April 15, 1946, to Kurt H. Wolff, reprinted in Wolff, "The Sociology of Knowledge and Sociological Theory" (1959), in Wolff, *Beyond the Sociology of Knowledge*; pp. 205–6.

31. Karl Mannheim, *Man and Society in an Age of Reconstruction* (New York: Harcourt, Brace, 1940), esp. p. 74, and *Freedom, Power, and Democratic Planning*. (It would be interesting to compare this book with David Riesman et al., *The Lonely Crowd*, which appeared in the same year, and Talcott Parsons, *The Social System*, of a year later.

32. Cf. *Surrender and Catch*, pp. 128–32.

33. Cf. Jürgen Habermas's "undistorted communication."

SEVENTH ENTRY
ANOMIE AND THE SOCIOLOGY OF KNOWLEDGE, IN DURKHEIM AND TODAY

Anomie and the Sociology of Knowledge, in Durkheim and Today

In entering the preceding entry, I said that it is the most personal one of all. It should now be clearer what this means. It does not mean "personal" in the mundane sense (the sense the term has in the world of everyday life); not, that I talk more about myself than elsewhere in this book, this venture. Although this is true, the sense of personal that does count for our sociology is *the blurring of the boundary between subject and object*, interpreter and interpretandum, myself and Mannheim. It would be quite a misunderstanding to speak here of prejudice, bias, lack of validation, arbitrariness. There is hardly anything arbitrary in the encounter with the phenomenon Karl Mannheim—surrender is the opposite of arbitrary, for it is necessary. In it, to repeat, one of the received notions that get suspended is the subject-object distinction. There (in the sixth entry, and in the whole book) there is the catch; now one could try to tease subject and object apart.

But at this point I feel called upon to return to the metaphor for the catch "Art Now?" (the second entry), which was rockbottom beginning, "fed by which further thinking could take off." The preceding observations on Karl Mannheim also urge further thinking, which, unlike that on the earlier occasion, is quite specific, namely, about explicating the place of subject and object in the sociology that is developing. But this, too, is for the future: I feel I don't yet have enough suspended notions to inspect the catch. In particular, there is at least one sociologist left who shaped both sociology and my own thinking: Emile Durkheim, and, in reference to our crisis, his most pertinent concept, anomie, particularly if we see it in relation to his sociology of knowledge.

I. Anomie and Sociology in Durkheim

What is this relation between the two, his *anomie* and his sociology of knowledge, that is, of intellectual-emotional phenomena; what is the relation between his worry about the one and his practice of the other? How can we account for his calling anomie by its name but his failing to *name* what he practiced, especially in the last pages of *The Elementary Forms of the Religious Life* of 1912, the term *Wissenssoziologie* being coined only a few years later, presumably by Max Scheler? Was he aware of normlessness but *not* of the sociology of knowledge as an approach he could take to account for anomie—anomie as just one of innumerable intellectual-emotional phenomena to be accounted for by reference to the social structure in which they exist? Was he so taken by moral problems that he failed to see normlessness as also a cognitive problem, as only one among uncountable others, and thus like all of them, a candidate for sociological analysis? Was he so passionately a moralist, as René König calls him,[1] that he failed to make a connection between a moral diagnosis and an intellectual diagnosis and to see that the latter could illuminate the former? Was he disproportionately taken by *conscience* as conscience rather than consciousness; was he thus also victimized by the French language? He did have an inkling of a new, social epistemology, above all in his effort to derive the categories of native Australian thought socially, but he seems not to have been aware of the extraordinary historical significance of such an epistemology as was carried much further by Karl Mannheim only a little more than a decade later.[2]

Although these are not rhetorical questions but questions that call for very specific study, I have not been able to undertake such study and thus must leave the questions almost entirely without answers. They are characteristic of the sociology here developing but are at least not predominant in the writers on Durkheim I have read:[3] here, as we know by now, the student is more involved, and more of the student is involved, than in the more customary studies in which the student more nearly observes and analyzes an object rather than interacting with another subject.[4]

II. Durkheim and Anomie

If I think of us (us human beings) today—I find it very difficult not to think of us human beings today: the thought is a *basso continuo*, a perpetual deep sound—I cannot help but feel that all preceding generations were unimaginably innocent compared to ourselves. Until now, the possibility of our and the earth's annihilation has been the monopoly of nonhuman nature, or of God, but our analysis and utilization of nonhuman nature has succeeded in changing that monopoly into a power which we now share with nonhuman nature. Since we have or are bodies that occupy space and have needs, we have always been part of nonhuman nature, that is (to repeat), we have always shared features with other animals and plants and nonorganic contents of the world: we have always been human only in part. What is new, as yet incomprehensibly new, is that our human, our exclusively human capacity, that capacity which has enabled us to create, among other things, science, has tilted the balance of the human-nonhuman synthesis that we are toward its nonhuman component and has thus given us an unprecedented nonhuman power. It is a benumbing case of the dialectic that has made us apprentices of our own sorcery.[5]

Thus, what does anomie mean today? Durkheim's idea or ideas about it can be no more than a slight prelude, if an ominous prelude. Durkheim applied the term to conditions he found in the France of his day; it referred to the division of labor gone out of control that characterized the burgeoning industrial society. It must have struck him as not threatening enough to prevent him from seeing the—unintended—irony of the word "organic" to designate that division of labor: at bottom, organic still referred to hardly more—the "hardly more," precisely, is anomie—than the division of labor typical of the second of two ideal types of society, that type in which he lived and which he had no choice but to approve, even though he was worried by the aberrations of the organic division of labor and of the suicide rate. Still, in comparison to our own situation, he appears as only one of a number of thinkers who, between the mid-nineteenth and mid-twentieth centuries, tried to come to terms with industrialization by contrasting the type of the industrializing societies in which he lived with a preindustrial type.[6] In comparison with the only six years younger Max Weber, Durkheim seems much less ascetic and much less explosive. He did participate in the institutional politics of his time; witness his writings on morality and education, and above all sociology, which he defended not only theoretically but succeeded in launching as an academic discipline. In comparison, Weber's passionate political interest found expression more in the daily press than in long-range plans for education and for the moral invigoration of his society.

III. Meeting Durkheim

The "sociological approach to the history of sociology" (the third entry) implies that its aim is to understand by reference to the society in which he or she lived now and why a given sociologist sees the world as he or she does. To this purpose, I must meet that sociologist, as I said in the case of Mannheim. But now we must examine what such meeting means. What does meeting another person mean, even if this person is no longer alive? This is not only a problem in the theory of intersubjectivity, such as it was posed by Husserl or Schutz:[7] I refer to the *experience* of meeting; I mean the question as an experiential question, and thus I can speak only for myself. Now I am on my way to Durkheim, on one of the ways I may have. On this way, at least, I feel that the desire for meeting him is motivated by the desire to survive *geläutert*—I cannot think of an equivalent English term that would connote all of cleaned or cleansed, purified, refined, but the root of *geläutert* is cleansed, washed clean. Of what? Of ignorance, uncertainty, confusion, error, so that reliable, certain knowledge is increased by the reappropriation, as Hans-Georg Gadamer[8] would say, following preceding received appropriations, other people's appropriations or reappropriations, of the phenomenon Emile Durkheim. And since a meeting is at issue, it is not only I who get cleansed, but the other whom I encounter does too. If that human being is alive, we both change in typically similar fashion, having new insights, understandings, feelings (which, of course, need not be the same for the two). But what could "cleansing" mean for the dead person? It must mean that in the encounter, because of the encounter, a new aspect or new aspects of the person or known aspects arrived at in a new fashion come into view; "cleansing" thus means an increment in the number and kinds of aspects under which the person is seen, understood, assessed, including the possibility of being dismissed, for however long it may be.

But when can we say that we have so met a person? How do we know that we have? I think of this as a pragmatic question, that is, a question the answer to which depends on the kind and degree of our desire to "survive the meeting *geläutert*." I know of no general equation with kinds and degrees of this desire as variables. In my own case, which I know better, the limits of my desire, in the present instance, are set by the focus on anomie and the sociology of knowledge, which is quite different from the aim to encounter Durkheim with no other focus, indeed trying to suspend whatever received notions, including expectations, I may have about him (in short, surrendering to him). The limits of my desire are also set, of course, by the brevity of the time at my disposal for this purpose, and finally by my comparative ignorance, the worse for poor memory.

IV. "Anomie" in Durkheim

I begin with anomie. I said that seen from our situation today, Durkheim's idea or ideas of it, whatever they were and could be, can be "no more than a slight prelude, if an ominous prelude." And this applies, and for the same reason, namely humanity's unprecedented situation today, also to all other conceptions and experiences of anomie and to the uses of the term. In ancient Greece, when the root of the term, *anomos*, "lawless" in the sense of "norm- or guidance-less," was coined, its meanings clustered around three major ideas: inhumanness, impiety, and injustice. This according to Marco Orrù,[9] who with Philippe Besnard[10] is one of the most thorough contemporary students of anomie. But Besnard calls "anomie" a "sign of professional membership" in the sociological community and thinks it "highly improbable that a test on another Greek word . . . could have caught the attention of a committee to select [articles] for a sociological journal." Furthermore, Besnard writes, "there can be no filiation between the Greek word and the use of the term anomie in the sociological literature. Never-mind, it is a matter of anomie, hence [it must be] sociology.[11]

It may well be true that no other Greek word has received as much attention in sociology as has anomie, and it may well be true that in France at least its use is a sign that one is a sociologist. But if it is so uniquely fascinating, surely there must be a reason for it. It might be that the word and what it stands for rings a bell, a bell that because of their particular sense of their time rings louder in the ears of sociologists than of other people. We know, Besnard argues, that Durkheim took the word from Guyau[12] but Besnard seems to exclude other influences as if there were no such thing as climate of opinion, spirit of a time, indeed a "collective consciousness" to carry it, and the word itself is no more than a catalyst, causing a shock of recognition. In fact, I suspect such a reaction both with reference to Durkheim and with reference to ourselves, rather than our interest in anomie being no more than that of members of the sociological community.

For Durkheim, surely, anomie was a problem not so much of sociology as of society, not so much a sociological as a social problem, and if as sociologists we are students of society rather than of sociology, it must for us, too, be a problem of society, of our society. Durkheim was worried about his France;[13] we are, or should be, worried about the whole globe; we should confront our worry. I suppose that with all his nationalist fervor,[14] Durkheim would participate in our worry, especially after he no longer had to spend so much energy on institutionalizing sociology.

What did he himself mean by anomie? I can do no better than quote, at some length, from Philippe Besnard's informative book:

The word "anomie" is rather rare in Durkheim's work. It appears with a certain frequency only in *La division du travail social* (1893), in the second preface to this book written in 1901, and in *Le Suicide* (1897). The term is practically absent from Durkheim's other writings. Besides its applications relative to Guyau . . . , we may note, in a review of a book by Westermarck, the expression "sexual anomie," used in the sense of a "complete absence of all matrimonial regulation." . . . The Word "anomie" does not figure in the courses given at the time of writing *Suicide* (*Le Socialisme*) or shortly thereafter (*L'Education morale, Leçons de sociologie*). At most, we may note an "anomic state" in the last of these courses.[15] But as the theme is developed there, these courses contain all kinds of equivalents: state of anarchy, state of irregularity [*irrèglement*], lack of organization [*inorganisation*], sickness of infinity [*mal de l'infini*], or, in *Le Socialisme*, also state of rulelessness [*dérèglement*], of excitement [*effervescence*], or manic agitation. . . . From 1902 on, the word disappears completely from Durkheim's work, and its theme becomes quite secondary.

Durkheim thus uses the term circumspectly, as one can see even in *Suicide*, where it appears more often than anywhere else. At the time of its first occurrences, it is accompanied by a kind of translation: "state of rulelessness or *anomie*" . . . , "state of crisis and anomie." . . . It is preferred as an adjective (anomic suicide) rather than as a noun and in this case it is usually specified according to one of the modalities of anomie (economic, domestic, conjugal, sexual anomie). . . . The noun "anomie" not accompanied by an equivalent or a specification thus is rarely used by Durkheim, even in *Suicide*. Perhaps this indicates uncertainty in regard to the precise meaning of the term.[16]

It probably meant all the things mentioned, depending on the context in which Durkheim wrote and felt. If so, this does not prove that there is not something common to all of them, that there is not a root meaning, that it is not possible to discover what might be called the essence of anomie. Why did Durkheim not only not find such an essential meaning, but why may he not have thought of looking for it?

V. Sociology of Knowledge: Durkheim, Scheler, Mannheim

To explore this problem, I turn to the sociology of knowledge, by which I mean the application of a sociological approach to intellectual-emotional phenomena. Durkheim takes a sociology-of-knowledge approach, perhaps most clearly in *The Elementary Forms of the Religious Life*, where, in his sociological passion, he, as it were, precipitously claimed the social origins of the very categories of thought[17] while stating, it seems incidentally, that "the categories change in different places and times":[18] he seems unaware of thus maintaining epistemological, that is, cultural and historical relativism. The two men who are usually considered the founders of the sociology of knowledge, Max Scheler and Karl Mannheim, on the contrary were highly conscious of the problem and the challenge of relativism in their own sociologies of knowledge.[19] Mannheim was much more aware than Scheler of the intimate connection between his preoccupation with the sociology of knowledge and the time in which he lived. "What we are concerned with here," Mannheim wrote on the third page of *Ideologie und Utopie* in 1929,

> is the elemental perplexity of our time, which can be epitomized in the symptomatic question: "How is it possible for man to continue to think and live in a time when the problems of ideology and utopia are being radically raised and thought through in all their implications?"[20]

Four years before *Ideologie und Utopie*, in "The Problem of a Sociology of Knowledge," he had inquired into the origin of the sociology of knowledge:

> If . . . we ask ourselves about *the ultimate, fundamental factors entering into the constellation which necessarily gave rise to the problem of a sociology of thought* [knowledge] in our time, the following four things appear worthy of mention:[21]

the "self-transcendence and self-relativization of thought," that is, the insight that thought is not autonomous but "subordinate to other more comprehensive factors"; an "unmasking thrust of relativization"; relativization to the "social sphere"; and the aim of imputing, not some, but all thought "to an underlying social reality."[22]

Thus, Mannheim sought and believed that he found what had happened and was happening in his time that could account for the emergence of the sociology of knowledge—even what "necessarily gave rise" to it. He was interested in trying to understand "what was going on." If he used the term anomie at all, it certainly was not a key term or even a technical term, and he might well have joined Besnard in considering it more confusing than useful because of the disagreement over its meaning. One might say that during the years when his main focus was the sociology of knowledge, he was less interested in definitions than in establishing the new venture and establishing it above all by such empirical studies as those of historicism and conservatism.[23] In this respect, his attitude toward it thus resembles Durkheim's toward sociology in general.

To repeat, Durkheim must not have been sufficiently upset by the many meanings of "anomie" to search for a denominator common to them all. Might his moral strength, as well as his eagerness to establish sociology, have given him a steadfastness which despite the crises he and his country went through, notably the "Dreyfus Affair,"[24] prevented him from *experiencing* the anomie surrounding him (think of Nietzsche by contrast!)? Did he keep himself from so experiencing it as to have to go beyond the remedies he proposed in social organization and education,[25] or to go elsewhere, into the existential questions raised by the sociology of knowledge, into its epistemological, even ontological thickets? Aside from his no doubt gratifying devotion to sociology, his own high morality must have continued to guide him; and on the other hand, his society must not have been disorganized to the point of engendering the degree of uncertainty, confusion, and helplessness that prevented both Scheler and Mannheim, though in very different ways, from developing a theory for overcoming relativism. Such a hypothesis may gain in plausibility if we recall that Durkheim did live in a period when there was no totalitarianism or atom bomb or mass disposal of human beings as "things" (how innocent Durkheim looks in his rule to study social facts as "things" in the "organic" society!)[26]—a time many of us, especially the younger, find difficult if not impossible to imagine. Mannheim, of course, knew totalitarianism and the holocaust and was still alive when Hiroshima and Nagasaki were destroyed by nuclear blasts, but I know of no response of his to these events of 1945; and after Hitler, his interest was wholly taken up by thinking about the planned society that would exclude totalitarianism from prevailing ever again.[27] In trying to think from the perspective of their times, it appears that for Durkheim, sociology, and for Mannheim, the sociology of knowledge, was the answer to anomie. And the two anomies they perceived were different, too, as were the criteria that led them to their discoveries: for Durkheim it was the area of social organization, especially social cohesion (see above all *Suicide*); for Mannheim, it was epistemology.

Surely under Mannheim's influence, I believed the sociology of knowledge to be the great and powerful clarifier of the anomie I sensed around me. More than thirty-five years ago, I wrote that the sociology of knowledge

> defines a new situation—one world and cultural relativism. Before this self-realization of the sociology of knowledge, the situation was merely new, profoundly fascinating and profoundly threatening. The sociology of knowledge therefore may be called an elucidation of a new experience man has had and is still having. Through it, man adapts himself to living in one world and transcends cultural relativism. This transcendence takes the direction of a view of himself as . . . forever challenging his own exploration.[28]

Six years later I still quote this approvingly and add, as another way of expressing it: "the sociology of knowledge transforms a new and shattering experience into a problem."[29] But then, there grew in me the idea of surrender, and gradually I came to understand a connection between this idea and its root experience, and the sociology of knowledge. I grasped this connection by reading the idea of surrender-and-catch as a response to relativism (which went beyond Scheler and Mannheim) and perceiving that the characteristic of the idea of surrender, which connects it with the sociology of knowledge among other conceptions of the world,

> is the demand to make conscious what has happened historically: the need for revising received notions; and to meet this need by suspending, and thus testing in the extreme situation of surrender, as many received notions as is humanly possible . . . [with] the "catch" . . . [being] the yield, result, harvest of the surrender.[30]

If sociology and social organization shaped in its image is the response, Durkheim's response, to anomic social structure, and the sociology of knowledge is the response, Mannheim's response, to epistemological anomie, the idea of surrender-and-catch is the response to the feasibility of our suicide and the destruction of our habitat.[31] To quote myself for the last time,

> we may also say that the sociology of knowledge is an extrinsic interpretation of its time, our time; surrender, an intrinsic one: the former is, advocates, and practices such an extrinsic (sociological) interpretation but needs the latter to overcome the relativism it encounters in its practice by its remembrance, rediscovery, reinvention, the catch, of what is common to all human beings, what is universally human.[32]

VI. Some of Durkheim's Advocacies and Neglects

In my effort to explicate the relation between anomie and the sociology of knowledge which I suspected in Durkheim (as well as more generally), I tried to surrender to this task, naturally within the limitations I mentioned. In the process, as I also pointed out, I had to try, and wanted, to meet Durkheim; and whatever else the outcome of my endeavor may be—the catch of my surrender to my task—one thing I am glad to feel distinctly and that I hope you feel, too, is that Durkheim has come closer as a fellow sufferer,[33] a fellow human being.

And this is good, because, if only on such a comparatively slight occasion, it transcends the discontinuity imposed on us by our unprecedented crisis: here, as before on the occasion of Max Weber (third entry), Max Scheler (fourth), Alfred Schutz (fifth), and Karl Mannheim (sixth), I tried to bring "the experience of my own society to bear on my reading of [these thinkers], because I am eager to learn about the continuity between [theirs] and mine—actually . . . phases of the same society." This from the second entry, on what I consider a sociological approach to the history of sociology—which, we may recall, implies three further continuities: the translatability of the interpretandum's universe of discourse into the interpreter's, the remembrance or realization of sociology itself, and, most important, the continuity of what unites all people of good will: "inspiration by the idea of a good society can unite us for survival."

But to take up, in particular, Durkheim again: what were his advocacies and his neglects? He advocated a better society than he saw around him,[34] one in which, for instance, anomie with its relations and consequences, such as a heightened suicide rate,[35] would be greatly reduced; he also advocated a sociology which, being scientific, thus a more reliable guide than any other approach to improving society, would be instrumental in furthering social amelioration. Indeed, *Suicide* is one of the most convincing arguments in favor of sociology itself, since no other approach studies suicide *rates*. But in his very battle for sociology, Durkheim shortchanged the subject; in his passion for the science of sociology, he neglected the essentially human features in favor of those men share with other animals. He (like most sociologists) only dealt with types of human beings (such as make up rates, for instance), not with individual human beings in their uniqueness. (See the fifth entry on Alfred Schutz, a sociologist who—unlike Durkheim, it would seem— was torn, even though probably without full awareness of it, as we have seen, between type and unconfusable individual.)

VII. Strength and Weakness of Surrender

I know, probably better than anybody else, that these reflections on Durkheim are only a beginning, and how much this beginning needs criticism and support. But here my feelings of having merely begun is quite different from that which I express in concluding my meditation on "art now?" (second entry). Then I felt

> I must not unduly suffer from the fact that I have not been able to say more on this occasion than I have, for the beginning I have made goes beyond itself, bearing on my life and your lives, whoever you are, unpredictably.

I could afford to be patient because I felt closer to that occasion of my surrender, the question of art now, than I did to the present occasion, anomie and the sociology of knowledge in Durkheim and today: that is, my feeling of here having merely made a beginning refers to Durkheim rather than to anomie or the sociology of knowledge, with both of which I am more familiar than with Durkheim. This shows that the degree to which a person can surrender to something or somebody depends, among other things, on that person's knowledge of what or who is being surrendered to and on the affective relation to it. And this is the weakness of the strength of surrender-to as a way of sociology and a way of life.

Notes

1. René König, "Emile Durkheim: Der Soziologe als Moralist," in *Klassiker des soziologischen Denkens, Band I, Von Comte bis Durkheim*, ed. by Dirk Käsler (Munich: Beck, 1976), pp. 312–64, 401–44.
2. Karl Mannheim, "On the Interpretation of 'Weltanschauung' " (1921–1922), in *Essays on the Sociology of Knowledge*, ed. by Paul Kecskemeti (London: Routledge & Kegan Paul, 1952), pp. 33–83; "The Problem of a Sociology of Knowledge" (1925), ibid., pp. 134–90; "The Sociology of Knowledge" (1931), in *Ideology and Utopia: An Introduction to the Sociology of Knowledge*, trans. by Louis Wirth and Edward Shils (New York: Harcourt, Brace, 1936), pp. 237–80; letter to Kurt H. Wolff (1946), in Wolff, *Trying Sociology*, pp. 557–9, and *Beyond the Sociology of Knowledge: An Introduction and a Development*, pp. 202–4.
3. Talcott Parsons, *The Structure of Social Action* (New York: McGraw-Hill, 1937), chs. 8–11; H. Otto Dahlke, "The Sociology of Knowledge," in *Contemporary Social Theory*, ed. by Harry Elmer Barnes, Howard Becker, Frances Bennett Becker (New York: Appleton-Century, 1940), pp. 66–71; Claude Levi-Strauss, "French Sociology," in *Twentieth Century Sociology*, ed. by Georges Gurvitch and Wilbert E. Moore (New York: Philosophical Library, 1945), pp. 503–35; Lewis A. Coser, "Emile Durkheim, 1858–1917," in *Masters of Sociological Thought: Ideas in Historical and Social Context* (New York: Harcourt Brace Jovanovich, 1971), pp. 129–74; Anthony Giddens, *Capitalism and Modern Social Theory*, part 2 (Cambridge: Cambridge University Press, 1971); *Studies in Social and Political Theory* (New York: Basic Books, 1977), chs. 6–9; Steven Lukes (1973), *Emile Durkheim: His Life and Work, A Historical and Critical Study* (Hammondsworth: Penguin, 1975); König, "Emile Durkheim"; Edward A. Tiryakian, "Emile Durkheim," in *A History of Sociological Analysis*, ed. by Tom Bottomore and Robert Nisbet (New York: Basic Books, 1978), pp. 187–236; Jürgen Habermas, *Theorie des kommunikativen Handelns*, Band 2 (Frankfurt: Suhrkamp, 1981), pages on Durkheim; Donald N. Levine, "Emile Durkheim: Universalist Manqué," in *The Flight from Ambiguity* (Chicago: University of Chicago Press, 1985), pp. 55–72.
4. See increasing explication in the following writings of mine: "Vilfredo Pareto" (1941), in *Trying Sociology*, pp. 5–16; "Introduction," in *The Sociology of Georg Simmel*, ed. and introd. by Wolff (Glencoe: Free Press, 1950), pp. xvii–lxiv; "The Challenge of Durkheim and Simmel" (1958), in

Trying Sociology, pp. 17–28; "Ernst Grünwald and the Sociology of Knowledge" (1965), ibid., pp. 591–608, and *Beyond the Sociology of Knowledge*, pp. 236–53; "Georg Simmel" (1968) in *Trying Sociology*, pp. 29–42; "Introduction: A Reading of Karl Mannheim," in *From Karl Mannheim*, ed. and introd. by Wolff (New York: Oxford University Press, 1971), pp. xi–cxi; "Karl Mannheim," in *Klassiker des soziologischen Denkens, Band II, Von Weber bis Mannheim*, ed. by Dirk Käsler (Munich: Beck, 1978), pp. 286–387, 489–97, 545–65; "Karl Mannheim: An Intellectual Itinerary," *Society* 21 (1984): 71–4; "Ein Zugang zu Simmel," in *Georg Simmel und die Moderne: Neue Interpretationen und Marerialien*, ed. by Heinz-Jürgen Dahme and Otthein Rammstedt (Frankfurt: Suhrkamp, 1984), pp. 174–7; "Versuch ze einem Karl Wolfskehl," in *Almanach 1986* (Darmstadt: Saalbau-Galerie, 1986), pp. 32–9; and this book.

5.   "Herr, die Not ist gross!   Lord, the trouble is great!
     Die ich rief, die Geister   The spirits I summoned
     werd ich nun nicht los."   I can't get rid of.
     (Goethe, *Der Zauberlehrling*)   (Goethe, *The Sorcerer's Apprentice*)

6. Some of these dichotomies are Henry Maine's "status" vs. "contract" (1861), Spencer's "military" vs. "industrial," Toennies' "*Gemeinschaft*" vs. "*Gesellschaft*" (1887), Howard Becker's "sacred" vs. "secular" (1930), Ralph Linton's "universal" vs. "alternatives" (1936), Robert Redfield's "folk" vs. "urban" (1947); cf. my "Some Considerations Preliminary to the Study of Social Change" (1963), in *Trying Sociology*, pp. 74–84.

7. Edmund Husserl, *Cartesianische Meditationen und Pariser Vorträge* (fifth entry, n. 18); Alfred Schutz, "The Problem of Transcendental Intersubjectivity in Husserl" (1957), in *Collected Papers*, vol. III, ed. by Ilse Schutz (The Hague: Nijhoff, 1966), pp. 51–84.

8. Hans-Georg Gadamer, *Truth and Method*, trans. and ed. by Garrett Barden and John Cumming (New York: Continuum, 1960).

9. Marco Orrù, "Anomie and Social Theory in Ancient Greece," *European Journal of Sociology* 26 (1985): 3–28; cf. Orrù, "Anomie and Reason in the English Renaissance," *Journal of the History of Ideas* 47 (1986): 177–96; *Anomie: History and Meanings* (Boston: George Allen & Unwin, 1987); "Weber on Anomie," *Sociological Forum* (1989): 263–70.

10. Philippe Besnard, *L'anomie: ses usages et ses fonctions dans la discipline sociologique depuis Durkheim* (Paris: Presses Universitaires de France, 1987). Also see Stjepan Meštrović and Hélène M. Brown, "Durkheim's Concept of Anomie as Dérèglement," *Social Problems* 33 (1985): 81–99.

11. Besnard, *L'anomie*, pp. 10–11.

12. Cf. Marco Orrù, "The Ethics of Anomie: Jean Marie Guyau and Emile Durkheim," *The British Journal of Sociology* 34 (1983): 499–518; cf. Giddens, *Capitalism and Modern Social Theory*, p. 80, n. 62.

13. Cf. Henri Peyre, "Durkheim: The Man, His Time, and His Intellectual Background," in *Emile Durkheim, 1858–1917: A Collection of Essays, with Translations and a Bibliography*, ed. by Kurt H. Wolff (Columbus: Ohio State University Press, 1960), pp. 3–31. König, "Emile Durkheim"; Lukes, *Emile Durkheim*; Tiryakian, "Emile Durkheim."

14. Emile Durkheim, *Who Wanted War? The Origin of the War according to Diplomatic Documents* (Paris: Colin, 1915) (trans. not indicated); "*Ger-*

many Above All": German Mentality and the War (Paris: Colin, 1915) (trans. not indicated).

15. In English: *Professional Ethics and Civic Morals*, trans. by Cornelia Brook-field, preface by H. N. Kubali and with an introd. by Georges Davy (London: Routledge & Kegan Paul, 1957).

16. Besnard, *L'anomie*, pp. 26–7.

17. Durkheim, *The Elementary Forms of the Religious Life: A Study in Religious Sociology* (1912), trans. by Joseph Ward Swain (1915) (Glencoe: Free Press, 1947), pp. 440–4; Durkheim and Marcel Mauss (1903), *Primitive Classification*, trans. and introd. by Rodney Needham (Chicago: University of Chicago Press, 1973); cf. *Durkheim: Selected Writings*, ed. and introd. by Anthony Giddens (Cambridge: Cambridge University Press, 1972), pp. 250–68.

18. Durkheim, *Elementary Forms of Religious Life*, p. 18.

19. Cf. Max Scheler, *Problems of a Sociology of Knowledge* (fourth entry, n. 2) Mannheim, "The Problem of a Sociology of Knowledge;" Kurt H. Wolff, "The Sociology of Knowledge and Surrender-and-Catch" (1982), in *Beyond the Sociology of Knowledge*, pp. 261–3; see also fourth and sixth entries.

20. Karl Mannheim, *Ideologie und Utopie* (Bonn: Friedrich Cohen, 1929), p. 3, or, moved by his translators to p. 38 of the "Preliminary Approach to the Problem," in *Ideology and Utopia*.

21. Mannheim, "The Problem of a Sociology of Knowledge," p. 126.

22. Cf. ibid., pp. 137–40.

23. Karl Mannheim, "Historicism" (1924), in *Essays on the Sociology of Knowledge*, pp. 84–133; "Conservative Thought" (1927), in *Essays on Sociology and Social Psychology*, ed. by Paul Kecskemeti (New York: Oxford University Press, 1953), pp. 74–164; *Konservatismus: Ein Beitrag zur Soziologie des Wissens* (1925), ed. by David Kettler, Volker Meja, Nico Stehr (Frankfurt: Suhrkamp, 1984); *Conservatism: A Contribution to the Sociology of Knowledge*, trans. by David Kettler and Volker Meja from the first draft by Elizabeth R. King, ed. and introd. by David Kettler, Volker Meja, and Nico Stehr (London: Routledge & Kegan Paul, 1986).

24. Cf. Lukes, *Emile Durkheim*, pp. 332–49.

25. Emile Durkheim, Preface (1902) to the second edition of *The Division of Labor in Society* (1893), trans. by George Simpson (Glenco: Free Press, 1947), p. 1–31; *Education and Sociology* (papers from 1903 to 1911), trans. by Sherwood D. Fox, foreword by Talcott Parsons (Glencoe: Free Press, 1956); *Essays on Morals and Education* (papers from 1904 to 1920), trans. by H. L. Sutcliffe, ed. and introd. by W. S. F. Pickering (London: Routledge & Kegan Paul, 1977); *Moral Education* (1925), trans. by Everett K. Wilson and Herman Schnurer, foreword by Paul Fauconnet, ed., with a new introd. by Everett K. Wilson (New York: Free Press, 1981).

26. Emile Durkheim, *The Rules of Sociological Method* (1895) *and Selected Writings on Sociology and Its Method* (papers from 1895 to 1917), trans. by W. D. Halls, ed. and introd. by Steven Lukes (New York: Free Press, 1982), ch. 2.

27. Karl Mannheim, *Man and Society in an Age of Reconstruction* (sixth entry, n. 31), *Diagnosis of Our Time: Wartime Essays of a Sociologist* (London: Routledge & Kegan Paul, 1943); *Freedom, Power, and Democratic Planning* (sixth entry, n. 28).

28. Kurt H. Wolff, "A Preliminary Inquiry into the Sociology of Knowledge from the Standpoint of the Study of Man" (1953), in *Trying Sociology*, p. 542, *Beyond the Sociology of Knowledge*, p. 187.
29. Kurt H. Wolff, "The Sociology of Knowledge and Sociological Theory" (1959), in *Trying Sociology*, p. 571, *Beyond the Sociology of Knowledge*, p. 216.
30. Wolff, *Beyond the Sociology of Knowledge*, p. 264.
31. Cf. Judith Feher, "On Surrender, Death, and the Sociology of Knowledge," *Human Studies* 7 (1984): 211–26.
32. Wolff, *Beyond the Sociology of Knowledge*, p. 266.
33. In *Emile Durkheim and the Reformation of Sociology* (Totowa, NJ: Rowman & Littlefield, 1988), Stjepan G. Meštrović, in part on the basis of interviews with Etienne Halphen, Durkheim's grandson, and Pierre Halbwachs, Maurice Halbwachs's son, writes of Durkheim in a much more specific sense as a "fellow sufferer," namely of his "obsession with suffering and unhappiness [, which] tends to be ignored by sociologists" (p. 2). See, e.g., Emile Durkheim, "The Dualism of Human Nature and Its Social Conditions," trans. by Charles Blend, in *Emile Durkheim, 1858–1917*, pp. 325–40; also Jerrold Seigel, "Autonomy and Personality in Durkheim: An Essay on Content and Method," *Journal of the History of Ideas* 48 (1987): 483–507, esp. 494–7.
34. Some of the most important among his many writings that are pertinent here are cited in n. 25; the most telling is probably the first (the famous Preface to the second edition of *The Division of Labor*).
35. Emile Durkheim, *Suicide: A Study in Sociology* (1897), trans. by John A. Spaulding and George Simpson, ed. and introd. by George Simpson (Glencoe: Free Press, 1951).

A TRANSFORMATION
OF THE ENTRIES:
FROM NOTHING TO SOCIOLOGY

A Transformation of the Entries: From Nothing to Sociology

I. Questions about Sociology

The task of answering our germinal question, how we can justify doing sociology at this time, has suggested, as we saw, a sociological reformulation of the history of sociology in more subjective terms, that is, the effort to understand, by reference to the society in which they lived, how and why particular sociologists have seen the world as they have; a glimpse at Max Weber and applications to Scheler, Schutz, Mannheim, and Durkheim have served to envisage such a more subjective history. But the reformulation involves two other questions—after the first which engendered our whole inquiry—namely, what are the strengths and weaknesses of such a sociological, "more subjective" approach to the history of sociology, and what is the bearing of this approach on the approach to sociology itself? These two questions are so intimately connected that they will be discussed as one.

Hence the next question is the third: what is the relation between this approach to the history of sociology and sociology, and the dominant if usually implicit view that sociology does not deal with individuals "as they actually are," but with types, ideal types, puppets—the view originally presented by Max Weber but, as we saw, rendered much more explicit by Alfred Schutz? Perhaps here it will strike us as plausible that this dominant view has something to do with the society in which it has grown to the point of being taken for granted—and if we do make this connection, we are adopting a sociological attitude toward sociology and thus once more instance what we said in response to the second question, that concerning the history of sociology: must we look at ideas of sociologists in reference to the society in which their ideas are found?

The dominant view of sociology as dealing only with types tends to ignore its fundamental flaw: that it omits meaning from its concerns other than as it itself constructs this meaning, inserts it into its ideal types, equips its puppets with it—that it is solipsistic. For since it does not deal with actual people, it cannot deal with either what they mean to themselves and others or with what the world or any part of it means to them. This failure to deal with meaning can be corrected and suggests a fourth question—why should it be corrected?

There is, however, another sense of the failure of sociology to deal with meaning, and this is a legitimate failure; it results from the fact that sociology only deals with temporal things—in the case of meaning, only with the rise, distribution, spread, strengthening, weakening, etc. of meaning during a given time at a given place. But how then does the sociologist, *qua* sociologist—and this is a fifth question—legitimately seek meaning?

It is clear that all of these questions—concerning the status of sociology, the history of sociology, its dealing with types, its failure to deal with meaning, the question of a sociology that deals with meaning—not only have to do with the possible justification of sociology but also logically precede sociology itself since they all issue from the problem of its justifiability. They are usually considered questions of the philosophy of sociology. But in advocating a sociological approach to the history of sociology and in urging such an approach on the occasion of recognizing puppets as the alleged subjects of sociology, there has been a hint already that these philosophical questions can be analyzed sociologically. This suggests a connection between such a sociological analysis and its society; thus we are witnessing the transformation of a philosophical into a sociological question. The last of our questions, the sixth, then, is whether we can generalize by saying that the history of sociology shows a movement from an earlier stage, dominated by the search for a philosophy of sociology, to a later stage, in which philosophy is approached sociologically. What now remains to be done is to take up these questions in so far as they have not been treated in the entries that precede.

II. Sociology?

Our seminal question, how to justify doing sociology in our unprecedented crisis instead of spending what energy we have on averting this crisis was our first entry—or, more precisely: our first entry into a conception of sociology that we trust is more commensurate with our crisis than are the sociologies that have remained unrevised by this crisis.

The worlds we entered in the examples of a sociology that made us leave that of everyday life, which nevertheless had raised the question of how to justify doing sociology, helped us recognize our everyday world, for today (see the end of the first entry) "we need to leave, get beyond, transcend the world of history, of everyday, if we would have any chance to recognize it." And if we

> trust our senses, rather than the received notions that blind them, and thus us, to reality, the only way we can come to terms with our "paramount reality" is to say "No" to it, as Herbert Marcuse put it, for " 'The whole is the truth,' and the whole is false."

There is more than one reason for such an attitude toward one's society. In the everyday world, in the "paramount reality," such an attitude (for myself) is protest against evil; in theory, it is the advocacy of suspending my traditions as best I can. This attitude expresses or at least suggests a relation to my time and place as something inevitable for sociologists, thus transferring us back to sociology's first century, referred to in the beginning of the first entry.

III. A Sociological Approach to the History of Sociology

All our entries have been entries into the *subject* as an approvable, desirable preoccupation of an approvable, desirable sociology. In the first entry, "Sociology?," we realized that the *subject* makes us forget our crisis, our time, history; and in the second, "A Sociological Approach to the History of Sociology," exemplified by a particular sociologist, Max Weber, the plea was for the *subject* as that toward which the history of sociology should be oriented. The *subject* was the preoccupation of the other entries, too—embodied by myself in the second entry ("Art Now?") and by Scheler, Schutz, Mannheim, and Durkheim, respectively, in the others.

The strength of this subject-inspired approach to the history of sociology and sociology altogether is that this approach (I argue at the end of the third entry)

> transcends the discontinuity imposed on us by our unprecedented crisis [by trying] to bring the experience of my own society to bear on my reading of [individual sociologists], because I am eager to learn about the continuity between [theirs] and mine . . . [And this implies three further continuities:] the conviction that the interpretandum's universe of discourse . . . can be translated into the interpreter's, . . . the remembrance or realization of sociology itself, [and] . . . the continuity of . . . all people of good will.

But what are the weaknesses of this approach? First, there is the danger that one's emotions—here illustrated by protest against evil, outraged by evil, hope, and whatever else they be and even if they cannot be tagged as simply—that one's emotions bias one's view, research, interpretation. But this is no worse than being biased or influenced by indifference, detachment, or "objectivity": in either case, the best we can do is try to be as aware of our own influence on our work as we can manage. The real weakness of the position sketched is not so much a weakness as a fact, namely, that it is inappropriate for many sociological investigations that indeed do not deal with individuals but, quite properly, with types or puppets.

IV. Sociology of Puppets

To make this clear requires a further distinction, in addition to that between unique human subject and (ideal) type or puppet. This is the distinction between an affective and a nonaffective ("affectively neutral," as Talcott Parson called it) attitude toward *either* individual *or* puppet. Let us recall the examples of sociology affirmed (first entry), and we find that all three of their authors exhibit an affective attitude toward their subjects: compassion, respect, sympathetic understanding in the study of Holocaust survivors, an effort to draw the reader into the machinist's world in the second study, and outrage and a persecutor's zeal in *The Perfect War*. The personae of the three studies, however, differ: they are (roughly speaking) unique human beings in the survivor study, but types in the other two. Nevertheless, all three convey to me the *subject* as the central concern of the sociology they represent. Accordingly, I must conclude that the subject may be either a unique individual or a type because either of them can exemplify the nature of man or the human condition. The fundamental feature of this sociology is that they convey what it *means* to be human ("human" in quite a "value-free" sense).

The question of unique individuals vs. puppets touches on a fundamental problem of intersubjectivity: the problem of whether I can know you other than as a type, albeit on a range from minimum to maximum in depth and detail, or whether it is possible for me to know you as you, and nobody else, really are (see the fifth entry). Max Weber and, developing him, Alfred Schutz have shown us what we did not know: that we even in the world of everyday life, and only more consciously and systematically as sociologists, exclusively deal with types—it is like the discovery that we have always spoken prose. But I have tried to show that Schutz, presumably without being aware of it, is ambivalent on this point. In an effort to account for this ambiguity I have suggested a conflict between asceticism and passion, which may remind us of a similar conflict in Max Weber, on which we touched in the third entry, and which alerts us to a discontent with society that also has found other expressions, such as Durkheim's anomie or Weber's ambivalence toward rationalization or Freud declaring this discontent to be of the essence of culture.

We, too, I believe, suffer from this conflict when we ask whether a sociology other than of types of puppets is possible. To me the answer is affirmative—an example of such a sociology is Henry Greenspan's study of Holocaust survivors (first entry). We transform the type into a human being when we try to identify with him or her, that is, see the type as an instance of man and, as we already said, search for meaning.

What then, finally, is the weakness of this approach to the history of sociology and of the sociology it exemplifies? It is its inappropriateness for those sociological studies that treat people as puppets, as objects— e.g., as objects of generalization—for instance, in survey research. And the justification of treating subjects as objects is that the human being is both, is a "mixed phenomenon," that is (to recall), that it has unique features, crucially meaning and the search for meaning—this is the human being as *subject*—and shared features, and in this capacity the human being is an *object*. A comprehensive conception of sociology must do justice to both, the human being as subject and as object. Survey research (and other investigations dealing exclusively with types or puppets) thus are justified, as long as their authors are not under the illusion that they are dealing with unique individuals. For if they think they are doing this, they merely engage in one of the many manipulatory exercises that characterize their society, but unlike propagandists and advertisers, they are not aware of it. They merely "do science," with a more or less undisturbed conscience.

V. Sociology and Meaning

Puppets, we recalled at the beginning of this entry, do not mean to themselves or to others and have no meaningful world; as long as it deals with puppets, therefore, sociology cannot deal with meaning. But we have seen ways in which sociology *can* deal with meaning: with its time, our time, with its history, with unique individuals. The presentation of such cases of dealing with meaning was, and is, inseparable from their recommendation as helping to overcome our discontinuity and as making us become clearer on whether we are dealing with unique individuals or with puppets and on the aims of each of these undertakings.

In an effort to clarify the relation between sociology and meaning, it is useful to remember Max Weber's definition of sociology:

> Sociology (as this very ambiguously used term is understood here) is to mean a science which wants to understand social acting interpretively and thus to explain it causally in its course and in its effects.[1]

Sociology wants to understand and thus to explain; it wants to grasp the meaning of something in order to explain it, that is, explain it causally: it wants to place meaning into a temporal frame. The examples of a sociology concerned with meaning that have been presented (in the first entry) do not go beyond the first of the two steps Weber's sociology is to take: understanding (or interpreting). They do not deal with temporal sequences. But after entering other worlds (the survivors', the machinist's, the Vietnam war's), sociologists must reemerge into the world of everyday life, the "paramount reality," to benefit it with their experience of the other worlds that absorbed them.

Here it is necessary to enter a distinction between two kinds of meaning, corresponding to the two human features, exclusive and shared, that characterize the human being: let us call them human meanings and social meanings. Social meanings can be understood sociologically within their own world, the everyday world; the sociologist does not have to leave it for another world. This is most easily seen in the case of what may be called social documents such as (typically) editorials, letters to the editor, advertising, as contrasted with (again typically), poetry, philosophy, painting, all of which transfer man into their own worlds. Thus,

> there is no sociology of religion but only of superstition, no sociology of knowledge but only of ignorance, or error, no sociology of art but only of kitsch (and I add [to this list by Albert Salomon[2]] philosophy, science, mathematics). . . . the reason is that all of these are, in their essence, *meaning*. Of course, there is the sociology of the church, the academy or bohemia, styles of poetry, schools of philosophy, universities and research institutes, and laboratories and thinktanks, discoveries in mathematics or logic. In short, there are sociologies of these intellectual-spiritual-emotional activities considered as *social institutions*. And the reason for this is that institutions are temporal and historical, and sociology can ask how and why they, or this or that one, came into being or didn't, developed or didn't, flourished or languished, were welcomed, supported, attacked by specific groups (and why by these), or disappeared. All of these are temporal matters.[3]

Now recall how Max Weber figured in the sketch of a sociological approach to the history of sociology (third entry). Of course Max Weber is "temporal" in the simple sense that he lived during a particular time. And we saw meaning in his work that illuminates our own time, the situation of humanity now. We did not try to account for the rise of the meaning "Max Weber" in a causal sense (such as he himself did with regard to the Protestant ethic): like the sociologists mentioned in the first entry, we stayed within the interpretive or understanding phase of Weber's two-phased sociology, not (even thinking of) entering the second, explanatory one.

To make this clearer, it may help to apply Karl Mannheim's distinction between intrinsic and extrinsic interpretation.[4] Intrinsic interpretation relies on the interpretandum as its only source; extrinsic interpretation goes outside the interpretandum in its effort to interpret it. Causal explanation is an extrinsic interpretation; in fact,

> causal explanations are not, properly speaking, interpretations, but determinations of un-meaning causal nexuses. They are concerned with the ascertainment of all those processes which, in themselves un-meaning, that is, not understandable, can merely be observed in their regularity; while they are preconditions, they are not presuppositions of the context of meaning to be interpreted.[5]

We need not accept Mannheim's view of the lack of meaning that he claims characterizes the observable processes that are the preconditions "of the context of meaning [the interpretandum] to be interpreted" and may rather emphasize that causal explanation is surely not "unmeaning," perhaps going as far as Alfred Schutz, for whom the adequacy of a causal explanation is a variant of the adequacy of a meaningful interpretation:[6] what matters here in our effort to envision an adequate sociology is that causal explanation is extrinsic to the interpretandum because it resorts to features of the cosmos (processes, laws) which, though at work in it (being "preconditions"), are foreign to it in their meaning (are not "presuppositions").

VI. From Philosophy of Sociology to Sociology of Philosophy?

1

The last of the six questions (at the end of I, this entry) concerns the relations between sociology and philosophy, more particularly the question whether in the history of sociology we can observe a shift from philosophy of sociology to sociology of philosophy. We must now formulate this question more precisely and begin with the relationship itself between sociology and philosophy.

The nature of this relationship as it figures here becomes clearer if we compare it with its conception by Georg Simmel.[7] For Simmel in his last analysis of sociology (1917), the center of this relation is a complex of questions "concerning the fact 'society.'" [8] This complex consists of two kinds of questions: epistemological, dealing with "the conditions, fundamental concepts, and presuppositions of concrete research," [9] and metaphysical, that is, those that

> ask where the neutral and natural sequences of events might provide these events or their totality with *significance*. . . . More particularly, they ask questions such as these: Is society the purpose of human existence, or is it a means for the individual? Does the ultimate value of social development lie in the unfolding of personality or of association? Do meaning and purpose inhere in social phenomena at all, or exclusively in individuals? . . .

> Evidently [Simmel points out], this type of question cannot be answered by the ascertainment of facts. Rather, it must be answered by interpretations of ascertained facts and by efforts to bring the relative and problematical elements of social reality under an over-all view. Such a view does not compete with empirical claims because it serves needs which are quite different from those answered by empirical propositions.[10]

"The study of the epistemological and metaphysical aspects of society" constitutes "philosophical sociology." [11] It is part of the "field of sociology" (the title of the first chapter of *Fundamental Problems of Sociology*), which also contains general and formal sociology.

There are striking static elements in this view. First, sociology has an apparently unproblematic or taken-for-granted center: society. Second, there is the spatial image, according to which epistemological questions "go beneath the concrete knowledge of social life," while metaphysical ones, "as it were, go beyond it." [12] Third, facts cannot answer epistemological or metaphysical questions, for they arise from (human) "needs which are quite different from those answered by empirical propositions." [13] (Simmel's own example of "philosophical sociology" is "Individual and Society in Eighteenth- and Nineteenth-Century Views of Life." [14]) The picture we get is that of an orderly world in which sociology and philosophy have their well-marked places. What matters here is not a critique or an endorsement of such a view but the realization that we no longer live in that world; we live in one in which, among many other things, the boundaries between sociology and philosophy have become problematic.

This might be expected in view of much that has happened since the first World War, toward the end of which Simmel wrote the passage quoted. In the beginning of this entry I suggested that a conception of the history of sociology, its dealing with types rather than actual people, its problematic relation to meaning, and the question of a sociologist dealing with meaning are problems that have to do with "the possible justification of sociology." They arise for me from this question of its justification; they logically precede sociology itself; for this reason, I referred to them as philosophical. We now see that they resemble Simmel's epistemological questions. Yet here (and now) their relation to sociology is quite different from what it is for Simmel. For Simmel, we have seen, they concern "the conditions, fundamental concepts, and presuppositions of concrete research." By contrast, here, their nucleus is the justifiability of sociology *at this time in human history*. We have found—we have experienced—that at this time in human history the very meaning of "the conditions, fundamental concepts, and presuppositions" of sociology can no longer be taken for granted as having a fixed relation to sociology.

In our undertaking, in fact, philosophy has intersected sociology all along. Thus in the first entry, we found that the examples of relevant sociology shared in all their differences.

> the insistence on the *subject*, the recall, the vindication, the celebration of the subject at a time when the subject has been made into a thing by bureaucracy, snuffed out by totalitarianism, and when it will be destroyed physically if the threat from which . . . [our question ("Sociology?")] issues becomes fact—the last fact.

But how did we hit on this which lay behind (or in Simmel's terms, "beneath" or "beyond")—behind not all that now goes by the name of sociology, but behind the sociology that did not strike me as irrelevant in the face of our crisis? It is clear that the distinction philosophical-empirical no longer holds in the way it did for Simmel—and probably did, and does, for the majority of sociologists and, probably, philosophers even today. The more ambivalent distinction, however, has a tradition in sociology, namely, the sociology of knowledge, which aims at sociologically accounting for the occurrence and fate of intellectual-emotional phenomena, including philosophy, by referring them to features of the society in which they exist.

In the third entry, a sociological conception of the history of sociology was illustrated in the effort to interpret certain characteristics of a sociologist, Max Weber, by connecting them with certain characteristics of his society; and this conception is again distinguished by the espousal of a "philosophical" proposition, namely, that the sociology and history of sociology which would be relevant today are characterized by "commitment to a good society," by the concept of a normative society, which "entails an affective attitude [toward it] and also supplies a criterion for judging societies, extant or past." The relation between the emphases on the subject and on a normative conception of society, as well as the diagnostic-critical nature of both emphases, ought to be clear: both are reactions against eminently "empirical" circumstances, the origin of their claims. Similarly, the three continuities implied by the conception of sociology and its history submitted at the end of the third entry show themselves as reactions to the discontinuity of our historical time and place.

In this entry, IV, "Sociology of Puppets," the relation between sociology and meaning is introduced: in contrast to people, puppets mean nothing to themselves or to other puppets and they live in a meaningless world; thus, sociology dealing with puppets encounters no meaning. It does, we found, if it considers either people or puppets as instances of humanity; but it does not when treating them (more accurately, when treating types or puppets) as objects for its own (or somebody else's) purposes. Here again, what underlies these determinations is a view of man (a "mixed phenomenon") adduced once again to account for (aspects of) empirical reality, including, if only implicitly, such features of our time and place as anonymity, loneliness, meaninglessness. In treating people as puppets, sociology repeats the treatment that many people more often than not experience and practice in our everyday world. Sociology thus connives in a prevalent value judgment and in a by no means morally neutral activity, which it denies but which the sociology here advocated denounces for the sake of a better society.

What the fifth section in this entry, "Sociology and Meaning," adds to the discussion in the preceding section is the distinction between social and human meanings. Social meaning is limited to the illumination of shared human features: many animals other than human beings are social or even live in societies, the difference between them and man being verbal language with all this entails. Thus practically all social relations among men are mediated symbolically, culturally, but nevertheless may be most realistically understood by reference to types of interaction found also among other animals. For instance, it would be erroneous or naive to read editorials, letters to the editor, or advertising "intrinsically," literally, rather than "extrinsically," as expressions of fight, partisanship, desire for power or influence, just as it would be mistaken to read a poem, a philosophical essay, or a painting (to remain here in both cases of meaning with the examples given in section V) only extrinsically rather than also, indeed first, intrinsically: first trying to understand, then if at all to "explain" (to recall again Max Weber's definition of sociology). The latter twofold procedure is that of the sociology of knowledge (which often is short on the intrinsic phase, as literary criticism often neglects the extrinsic one).[15]

Both conceptions here suggested of sociology and of the relationship between it and philosophy—understood as dealing with the foundational problems of sociology—are obviously based on an assessment or diagnosis of this time in human, possibly planetary history, and this diagnosis itself is couched in the same terms that have been applied to the history of sociology advocated. The sociology involved is more dynamic than more customary sociologies in that it questions past self-understandings of sociology and, in the sense in which the crisis of humanity is unprecedented, does with far fewer "precedented" concepts and theories, calls into question, "suspends," "brackets" many of them—in fact, as many as possible, or more accurately, as many as bearable. In other words, it *surrenders to* the question of its justifiability at this time.

2

What, then, of the sixth question, whether in the history of sociology we can observe a shift from philosophy of sociology to sociology of philosophy? What is here suggested is that there have been two such shifts. The first came with the insight that the historical fate of philosophical problems can be accounted for sociologically—the achievement of the sociology of knowledge, which at its best resists sociological reductionism, or sociologism, that is, the temptation to see the meaning of philosophical (and other) problems exclusively in the socio-historical circumstances, to commit the genetic fallacy, which claims that origin determines validity.[16] The second step is the recognition of the unprecedented crisis as the basis of human endeavor, including sociology and philosophy, which thus change in their mutual relation in ways exemplified here throughout and particularly in the present section. "From philosophy of sociology to sociology of philosophy" is good rhetoric but untenably inaccurate. Its truth is the affirmation of a second step in the "secularization" of thinking these pages embody. Short of the ultimate catastrophe, there will always be—though not everywhere and not every moment (dependent on the political situation in the broadest sense of the term)—both philosophizing about sociology and sociological analysis of philosophy. What distinguishes *this* phase in the history of the two enterprises and their relation is this "second step"—a new step.

Almost sixty years ago (see the sixth entry) Karl Mannheim argued for the secularization which is at issue here and which is still today a matter of passionate dispute. But he first disavowed the sociologism that serves as an excuse for not facing this secularization. A sociological interpretation, he wrote (to repeat), does not imply

> that mind and thought are nothing but the expression and reflex of various "locations" in the social fabric, and that there exist only quantitatively determinable functional correlations and no potentiality of "freedom" grounded in mind; it merely means that even within the sphere of the intellectual, there are processes amenable to rational analysis, and that it would be an ill-advised mysticism which would shroud things in romantic obscurity at a point where rational cognition is still practicable. Anyone who wants to drag in the irrational where the lucidity and acuity of reason still must rule by right merely shows that he is afraid to face the mystery at its legitimate place.[17]

Thus, there is no denying mystery—or validity; secularization does not mean wholesale debunking but only debunking "romantic obscurity." The "second step" has been made possible by the power of technological developments, such as the nuclear forces, to destroy us. Hence, among myriad other questions, the question of "Sociology?," the pursuit of which has led to the topic of our last subhead, "from philosophy of sociology to sociology of philosophy?" We have found that in its literal sense it is a nonsense question, the truth of which, however, is that among the many received notions that we must suspend at this time in our history is also the notion that sociological and philosophical problems are qualitatively so different as to be mutually irrelevant. Instead, at this stage of our inquiry, we must examine each case on its own merits, rather than assuming an answer.

The general idea behind these pages is the idea of surrender-and-catch, particularly its advocacy of the suspension, to one's best ability, of received notions, with the catch unforeseeable. In the present instance, the first catch of my surrendering—our surrendering—to the question of sociology's justifiability today are these pages. My hope, of course, is that other sociologists will ask and answer the question "Sociology?" in their own authentic ways and that still others will ask and answer it in respect to their own disciplines, since the "question raised about sociology applies, of course, to all human activities" (see the first entry). May we seize the chance of facing it in the unprecedented sense that our unprecedented turning point in history has given it.

Notes

1. Max Weber, *Economy and Society* (1911–13), ed. by Guenther Roth and Claus Wittich (New York: Bedminster Press, 1968), vol. 1, p. 4 (translation slightly modified).

2. Albert Salomon, "Prophets, Priests, and Social Scientists" (1949), in *In Praise of Enlightenment* (Cleveland and New York: Meridian Books, 1963), pp. 387–98.
3. Wolff, "Exploring Relations between Surrender-and-Catch and Poetry, Sociology, Evil," *Human Studies* 9 (1986): 347.
4. Karl Mannheim, "The Ideological and the Sociological Interpretation of Intellectual Phenomena" (sixth entry, n. 15).
5. Ibid., p. 129 and n. 16 on Weber's view, the source of Mannheim's.
6. Alfred Schutz, *The Phenomenology of the Social World* (fifth entry, n. 10), secs. 45 and 46, pp. 229–36, esp. p. 234.
7. Georg Simmel, *Fundamental Problems of Sociology* (1917), in *The Sociology of Georg Simmel*, trans., ed., and with an introd. by Kurt H. Wolff (Glencoe: Free Press, 1950), pp. 1–84.
8. Ibid., p. 23.
9. Ibid.
10. Ibid., p. 25.
11. Ibid., p. 23.
12. Ibid., p. 24.
13. Ibid., p. 25.
14. The title of the fourth (last) section of *Fundamental Problems*, pp. 58–84. For the development of Simmel's view of science and philosophy and their relations, see Heinz Jürgen Dahme, "Das 'Abgrenzungsproblem' von Philosophie und Wissenschaft bei Georg Simmel," in *Georg Simmel und die Moderne*, ed. by Heinz Jürgen Dahme and Otthein Rammstedt (Frankfurt: Suhrkamp, 1984), pp. 202–30.
15. For more on intrinsic and extrinsic interpretation, their relations, and the historical decline of the former, see Wolff, "Exploring Relations," 358–60.
16. Wolff, *Beyond the Sociology of Knowledge*, pp. 175–7.
17. Karl Mannheim, "Competition as a Cultural Phenomenon" (1928), quoted in the sixth entry.

Sources and Acknowledgments

The author gratefully acknowledges the following publishers and publications for permission to use previously published papers, which have been shaped to make of them a whole.

First Entry: "Sociology?," in *Social Theory and Social Criticism: Essays for Tom Bottomore*, ed. by William Outhwaite and Michael Mulkay (Oxford and New York: Basil Blackwell), 1987, pp. 10–16;

Second Entry: "Art Now?," *Kairos* 1, 4 (1985): 72–81;

Third Entry: "A Sociological Approach to the History of Sociology," *Journal of the History of the Behavioral Sciences* 21, 4 (1985): 142–44;

Fourth Entry: "Scheler's Shadow on Us," *Analecta Husserliana* 14 (1983), pp. 123–21;

Fifth Entry: "Into Alfred Schutz's World," *Analecta Husserliana* 26 (1988), pp. 73–84;

Sixth Entry: "The Idea of Surrender-and-Catch Applied to the Phenomenon Karl Mannheim," *Theory, Culture & Society* 5 (1988): 715–34;

Seventh Entry: "Anomie and the Sociology of Knowledge, in Durkheim and Today," *Philosophy and Social Criticism* 14, 1 (1988): 51–67;

A Transformation of the Entries: Part of (pp. 330–9) "From Nothing to Sociology," *Philosophy of the Social Sciences* 19 (1989): 321–39.

Index